The Concept of Dynamic Preparation

1. "Before anything else, *preparation* is the key to success."
   —Alexander Graham Bell

2. *Dynamic, adj.* Marked by usually continuous and productive activity.
   —Merriam-Webster

Dynamic Preparation—a term you'll see repeatedly in this book—is a powerful concept with various applications to the study of the classical guitar. So, what does it mean? Well, look again at the quotes above—the twin reference points which frame its meaning. It's a state of mental and bodily readiness that makes all physical actions easier and more efficient than if initiated "cold" from a more passive state of mind and body. For example, consider a batter waiting for a pitch, a tennis player anticipating the serve, or even a pet cat crouched and ready to pounce on a mouse toy. In all such cases, the muscles needed to move quickly and effectively at the right moment are being *primed* by mentally anticipating the upcoming movement.

The phenomenon of **priming** was discovered by physiologists in the 1930s, and research since then has proved its value in performing reflex-based tasks or learning new psychomotor skills. Although sports performance is the most obvious area of application, music performance is no exception. That's why you'll find lots of references to priming in the teaching literature under headings such as visualization, movement imagery, mental anticipation, aim-directed movement, seeing with the mind's eye, and so forth. The concept of dynamic preparation embraces all these meanings, and *dynamic preparation is the key to a superior classical guitar technique.*

Let's start with how you change chords, and consider each change as a journey from point A to point B. Like all trips, exactly *how* you'll get there is important, so having a good route in mind before you leave makes more sense than just relying on your sense of direction and luck to get where you want to go efficiently. In other words, having a clear mental image of *how* to get from one chord to the next beats merely relying on unthinking reflex movements drilled in by rote practice. Based on Gerhard Mantel's groundbreaking insights into mastering the cello—whose size, shape, and demands on the left hand are similar to those of the guitar—the most appropriate term for fingerboard movements based on laser-focused mental imagery is ***Goal-Directed Movement (GDM)**. The secret of GDM is to "see" the constantly changing fingerboard formations in the mind's eye as clearly as chord diagrams, and the most graceful, efficient way to get from one to another as clearly as a road map.

Grace and efficiency go together like a pair of shoes—i.e., the one implies the other. For example, consider how the slow-motion replays in TV sports broadcasts demonstrate this correlation for all to see. Movements which in real time appeared frantic—a diving pass-catch, a surprise layup, a winning overhead smash, a perfect Triple Lutz—look as fluid and graceful as underwater ballet when played back at half speed. What this means is great news for classical guitarists! By reverse-engineering the process and practicing for graceful efficiency of movement in "super slo-mo," as described on the next page, you'll instill conditioned reflexes that add up to a confident, relaxed style of performance at much higher speeds.

*See Gerhard Mantel, *Cello Technique: Principles and Forms of Movement* [1965], tr. by Barbara Thiem (Bloomington: Indiana University Press, 1975), "Part One: Goal-Directed Movement," pp. 3–40.

For an illustrative example, take the common G-C-D7-G chord sequence shown below in notes and chord diagrams. Read through it a few times to commit it to short-term memory. Then practice it cyclically—G-C-D7-G, G-C-D7-G, etc.—following the steps listed below.

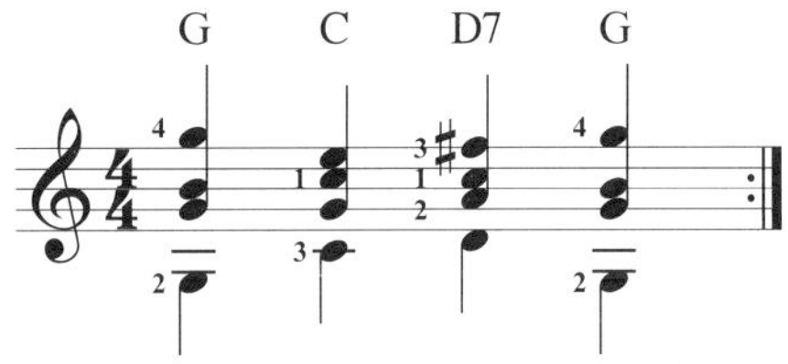

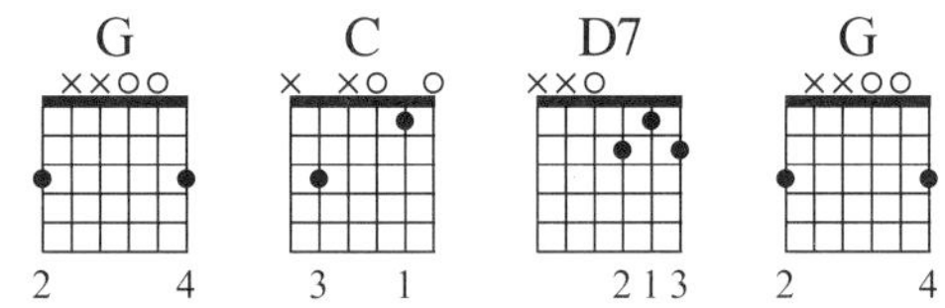

[1] Play very slowly—less than half tempo—and don't try to follow a beat. Allow enough time between movements to concentrate on their *movement style*, not just their target chord.

[2] Play *softly*. Because of the sympathetic neural linkage between the hands, the left hand naturally tends to work harder when the right hand plays more forcefully.

[3] Have a clear *mental* image of the next chord formation *before* releasing the one just played. Look at the frets the new chord will occupy; visualize the exact shape the chord will take and the exact form of movement needed to get into the new formation.

[4] Release the fingers but *don't* relax them *fully*. Keep their curvature, with the tips pointed at the fingerboard, while repositioning the hand and *molding* the fingers into the new chord shape.

[5] Then, as if the fingers were pegs dropping gently into holes drilled to receive them—like some classic Playskool toys—press down the strings and play the chord. Press *no* harder than needed to hold the notes cleanly and securely—don't "kill" the strings the way many players do in the mistaken belief that it's the right way to play.

[6] Practice until each hand position and chord shape appears to flow *seamlessly* into the next, just like the bodily movements in those "slo-mo" replays of exciting moments in ball games and competitive individual sports like tennis and figure skating.

This invaluable practice technique should be used for all the pieces and exercises throughout the book. Although there are others we'll study, GDM is the single most important form of dynamic preparation for the left hand. When you've mastered it and can use it confidently to learn new pieces as well as practice, it will provide a quantum leap in your *overall* technique.

Exactly the same may be said of the dynamic preparation techniques for the *right* hand you'll also learn in this book, which begins next. If all this is new to you, don't worry. Just follow the step-by-step directions carefully, be patient, and you'll be very pleased with the results—in fact, maybe even amazed.

DYNAMICALLY PREPARED FINGER-STROKES AND HAND POSITIONS

Right-hand finger-strokes are dynamically prepared by seating the nail(s) firmly against the string(s) and taking up some string-slack *before* executing the strokes. You can compare this process with archery: **(1)** the **preparation** is like notching and partly drawing an arrow; **(2)** the **execution** is like completing the draw and releasing it. Most commonly known as "planting," preparation yields benefits such as accuracy, efficiency, good tone, and speed. It's also the key to a **legato** style of playing in which the notes seem connected like tiny links on a fine gold jewelry chain.

2ND EDITION

A MODERN APPROACH TO CLASSICAL GUITAR

By CHARLES DUNCAN

Book 3

Photography by Douglas Niedt

Audio Recordings (for Book 3/Audio version 365530):
Performed by Judy Handler
Recorded and Mixed by Mark Levesque

ISBN 979-8-3501-6661-3

HAL•LEONARD®
A Muse Group Company

Visit Hal Leonard Online at
www.halleonard.com

World headquarters, contact:
Hal Leonard
7777 West Bluemound Road
Milwaukee, WI 53213
Email: info@halleonard.com

In Europe, contact:
Hal Leonard Europe Limited
Dettingen Way
Bury St Edmunds, Suffolk, IP33 3YB
Email: info@halleonardeurope.com

In Australia, contact:
Hal Leonard Australia Pty. Ltd.
4 Lentara Court
Cheltenham, Victoria, 3192 Australia
Email: info@halleonard.com.au

PREFACE—From Intermediate to Advanced Playing

If you've completed Book Two of this method or were already at that stage of development, you're ready to move up to a level defined by the best players. This means that you'll be learning some valuable new techniques that require good practice habits and patience to develop.

This new edition of Book Three will introduce you to those techniques in detail and provide plenty of exercises and music to develop them. If at all possible, you'll also need to be playing with fingernails as explained in Book Two (pp. 62–64). The use of nails is now universal and, with few exceptions, good players use nails filed and shaped as illustrated there.

Some techniques and concepts introduced in this new edition include the following:

- Mental anticipation as the key to accurate and efficient technique
- Goal-directed left-hand movements
- Dynamic stroke preparation, known generally as "planting," and its value for good tone
- The use of dynamic stroke preparation in playing arpeggios ("simultaneous planting" and "sequential planting")
- Precise coordination (i.e., synchronization) of the right hand with the left
- The development of confident, reliable speed in scale playing
- The "secrets" of optimal barred chord and slur technique
- The *real* secret of effortless, efficient fingerboard position shifting
- The techniques and uses of damping

As in the first edition, Book Three provides introductions to the remaining commonly used keys, the upper fingerboard positions, the techniques of artificial harmonics and flamenco, and more. The music includes solos from several periods, some of the author's compositions, and duets to enhance the study of the upper fingerboard.

Like the section on fingernails in Book Two, the genesis of many concepts and techniques in this book can be found in the author's *The Art of Classical Guitar Playing* (Summy Birchard Music, 1980)—a book which has had widespread influence on guitar teaching and playing for decades. In *this* book, they've been further developed, clarified, and methodized for easy and effective use by 21st-century students and their teachers.

I'm grateful for having been provided this golden opportunity to update my ideas in a fresh new format, and also for the synergistic input from the fine students who helped me "road-test" it. Many thanks also to the master teacher-performers who generously read the manuscript and made valuable suggestions for its improvement—Douglas Niedt, Frank Koonce, Louis Lawlor, Michael Jones, and Judy Handler. A special debt of gratitude is due to Judy for her superb recordings of all the pieces for the book/audio version of Book 3 (Hal Leonard 365530). A well-degreed protégé of legendary guitarist Oscar Ghiglia, she teaches in Connecticut and performs extensively with her husband Mark Levesque, who also did a masterful job with the recording.

And now let's get started!

Preparing and executing are defined also by how nails engage the strings during a stroke. As shown below, there's a **contact** point (C) and a **release** point (R). The flesh contact—from *above* the string only—serves to cushion the nail contact. The contact point for *i, m,* and *a* is near the thumb-side edge and the release is near the center, as seen in illustrations 1 and 2 below. For *p*, it's just the opposite: contact in the *middle* and release near the *outside* edge, as in illustration 3.

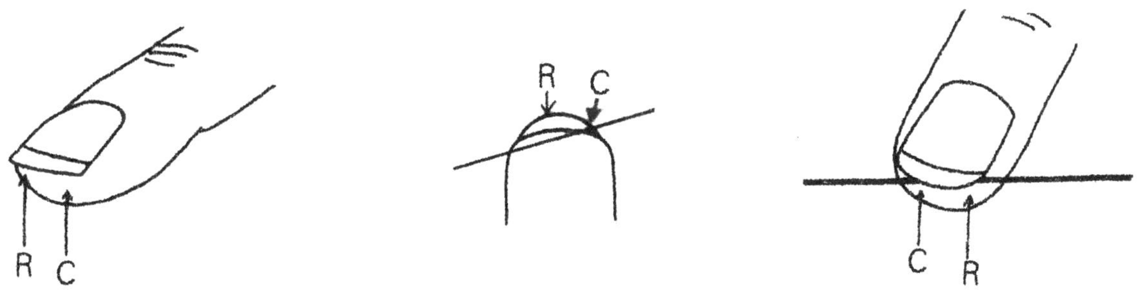

(1) (2) (3)

Fingernail seen from left side (1) and beneath (2), and thumbnail from above (3).

The three illustrations below show what dynamically prepared hand positions will look like to you:

(1) In the *right*-hand position, note how *p-i-m-a* have been molded into a compact playing unit. The thumb operates most efficiently when tucked in as shown, with the tip turned back, while the **lateral compression** of the fingers counters their common (and harmful) tendency to splay. This position also enhances right-hand stability, accuracy of touch, and consistency of tone color.

(2) The dynamically prepared *left*-hand position is just the opposite. With your fingers *already* hovering over the fret spaces like this, finding and holding notes is much easier than when the fingers aren't curved and spaced in this ready-to-play position. If you practice them conscientiously, the scale and slur exercises in this book will make it feel quite natural.

(3) The last illustration shows the natural alignment of hand, wrist, and forearm that you get when you make a fist. Since leverage and energy are transmitted most efficiently from the arm to the fingers when they're well-aligned, the fist provides a good conceptual model for *both* hands.

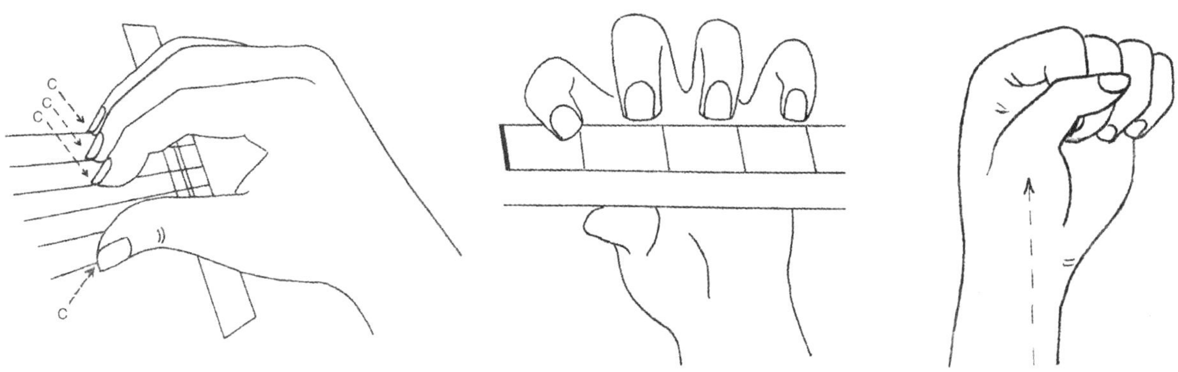

(1) (2) (3)

(1) The right hand on the strings in a planted, ready-to-play position with nails locked on. (2) The left hand in first position with the first finger on C and the others hovering over the fret spaces. (3) The natural alignment of hand, wrist, and forearm when the hand is comfortably in a fist.

In the next four-page unit, we'll explore the specific dynamic preparation techniques for the *right* hand which lay a foundation for instrumental mastery.

Dynamically Preparing Rest and Free Strokes with *p*:

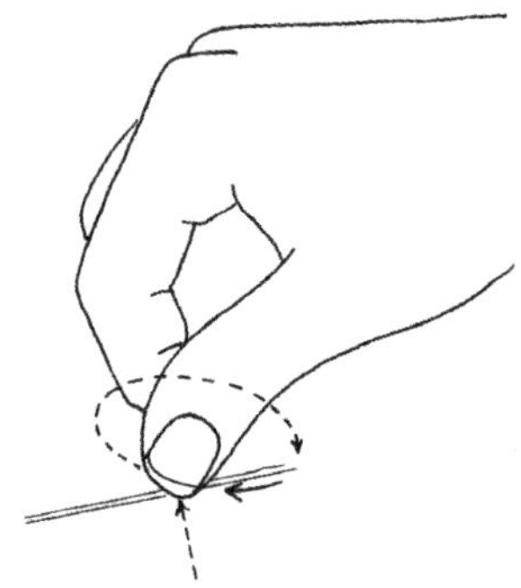

(1) With *i-m-a* planted to anchor the hand, plant *p* on the fifth string. Your hand should now look like the illustration on the previous page.
(2) For rest strokes, push down and to the right with *p* until it glides off the fifth string and comes to rest naturally against the fourth.
(3) For free strokes, use less downward pressure so that *p* barely clears the fourth string and recovers naturally by making a shallow return loop, as if it were bouncing back onto the fifth string.
(4) For both types of stroke, the force should come mainly from the basal joint at the wrist, not from flexion at the mid-joint or tip-joint.

Dynamically Preparing Rest and Free Strokes with *m-i*:

(1) With *p* planted on the fifth string for support, plant *m* on the B string.
(2) For rest strokes, push down and in until *m* glides off the string and comes to rest naturally against the G string. Then do the same with *i*.
(3) For free strokes, aim more toward the palm of your hand so that *m* and *i* barely clear the G string. As shown by the illustration, a good free stroke is more of a downward thrust from the knuckle than an upward pluck.

Dynamically Preparing Your Chord-Strokes:

(1) With illustration 1 on the previous page as a model, plant *p-i-m-a* on open strings 4–1.
(2) Take up the string-slack, balancing the pressure from *i-m-a* with equal force from *p*.
(3) Complete your stroke with a down-and-in "squeeze" that discharges the energy in the partly flexed muscles and feels like a release of tension. The *recovery* should return *p* to its starting point and leave *i-m-a* hovering over the strings, *not* aimed into the palm of your hand.
(4) Practice also with strings 5 and 6 as the basses and listen closely for consistent tone quality and volume.

Correcting a Faulty Position with Lateral Compression

Pictured below are four common variants of right-hand position (a, b, c, and d) that will spoil your efforts to put the instructions above to good use. Each is the product of *dysfunctional* muscular tension, as opposed to the *functional* tension needed to compress the hand into the compact playing unit illustrated on the previous page, with the thumb at about a 45-degree angle to the strings rather than nearly parallel, when the wrist is collapsed as in illustration (d).

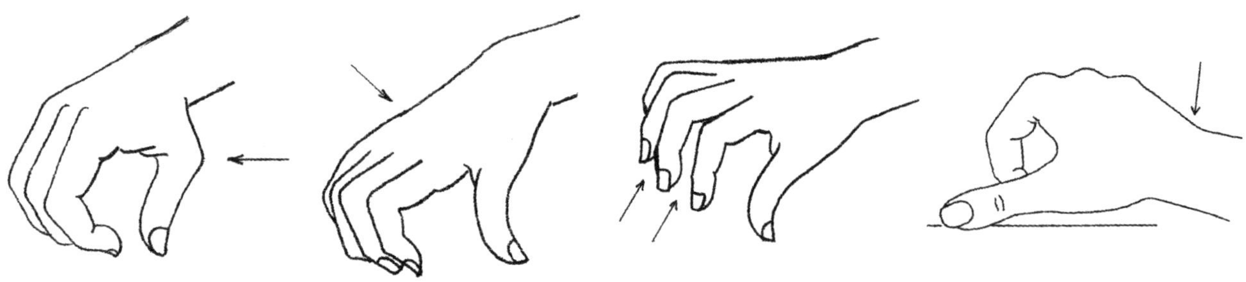

(a) *(b)* *(c)* *(d)*

The easiest way to form the correct position is by *laterally compressing* the hand muscles to grip a Ping-Pong ball within your palm as shown to the right. In fact, even a piece of printer paper crumpled into a little ball will serve the purpose just as well. You can actually play quite a bit while gripping the ball, but the real value of this training aid is to mold the hand, thumb, and fingers effortlessly into an optimal position as shown here from your point of view when playing.

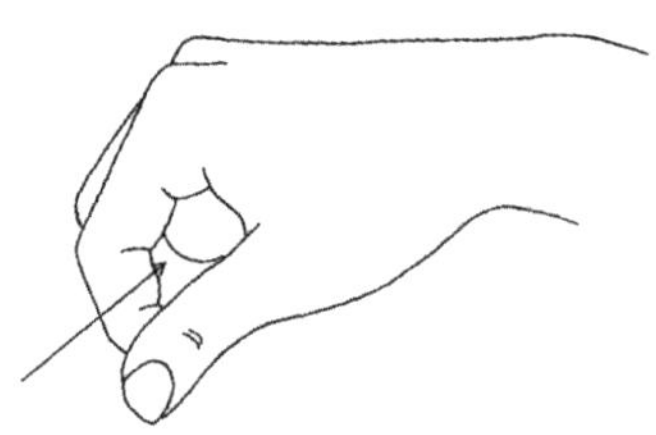

(e)

STACCATO PRACTICE

Dynamically prepared strokes are mastered by cutting notes short with **staccato** articulations. This will transform the practice techniques described earlier into conditioned reflexes and lay the foundation for truly **legato** playing. To learn this practice technique, just follow the "plant-play" prompts in the open-string exercises below, *preparing* on the rests and *executing* on the notes. This will create a moderately staccato effect by cutting the note durations in half.

Also, keep in mind the archery analogy from earlier—most of your effort should be expended on the preparations as you seat your nail(s) firmly and put tension on the string(s). Each time you do that, you minimize the effort needed to complete the stroke(s), and therefore the actual execution will feel more like a release of tension than a plucking action.

With *m-i* Rest Strokes, as in Scale Playing:

[1] Plant *p* on the fifth string and leave it down to anchor your hand.

[2] Plant *m* on the second string and play the B.

[3] Exactly as *m* comes to rest against the G string, plant *i* on the B string.

[4] Play the B with *i* and continue by preparing strokes on the *rests* ("plant") and completing them on the *notes* ("play").

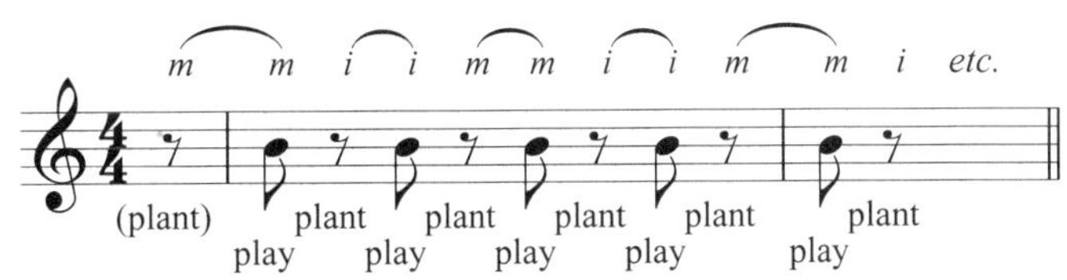

TIP: Don't think of the fast-planting movement as a separate, additional effort. It's triggered and assisted by the finger's natural reflex recovery from its preceding stroke, just like the footsteps when you walk. Consequently, with just a bit of good practice, the simultaneous "plant-play" exchange movement will feel as natural as walking.

With Chords:

[1] Do likewise with staccato *chord* practice by using your natural recovery from one chord-stroke to plant quickly for the next. This will cut the note values by half, except for the bass strings when you change from one to another.

[2] If the change is from string 5 to 4, or 6 to 5, you can **damp** the lower string with the left side of your thumb-tip as you plant on the higher string. As symbolized by the small arrow on each side of the "plant" prompt, just modify your preparation slightly so that the thumb-tip is *sandwiched* between the strings for an instant as the nail is being seated. (Damping a *higher* bass string is a more advanced technique you'll learn later [pp. 46–47].)

COORDINATING (SYNCHRONIZING) THE LEFT AND RIGHT HANDS

Staccato practice also works like magic to coordinate your hands by synchronizing their movements precisely. The secret is to overlap your *left*-hand finger action with simultaneous *right*-hand preparations that mute the string(s) temporarily. Then, you complete the stroke(s) at the moment the new note or chord is pressed down and recover by planting for the next note or chord. That will also trigger the *left* hand's next movement, so that the result is a succession of dynamically paired reflex movements which are synchronized together like windshield wipers.

The prompts in the exercises below, combined with the four-step approach to mastery for each of them, will accustom you to this invaluable style of practice. If it seems awkward or confusing at first, don't worry. Just follow the prompts and let your autonomic nervous system do the rest.

With Chords:

To learn synchronized chord-changing, use the easy A minor chord progression below.

[1] With *p-i-m-a* already planted on the correct strings, play the initial Am chord.

[2] On the rest ("plant/change"), plant for the Dm and make the chord change while the strings are damped. Be sure your thumb plants on the bass string for the *new* chord, not the one just played.

[3] On the next beat ("play"), play the Dm and recover by planting for the Am with E bass.

[4] Do likewise for each subsequent chord change, and repeat. Use the left side of your thumb-tip to damp string 5 on the change from Am to Dm and string 6 on the change from E7 back to Am.

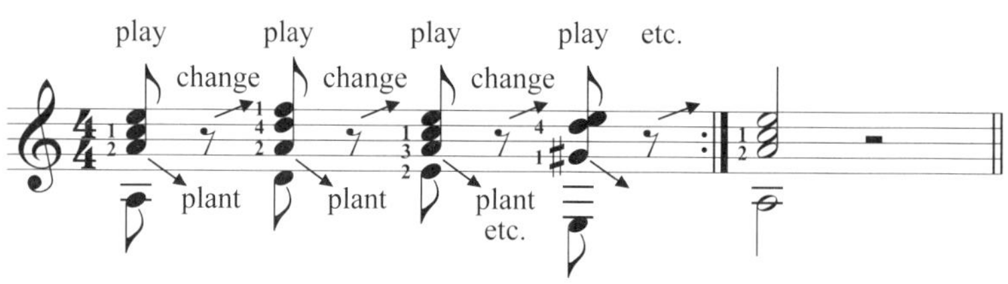

With *m-i* Scales:

[1] In scale practice, coordinate each left-hand finger's "attack" (or "fretting" of the next note) with the right-hand finger's plant for the note—in the chromatic scale pattern below, *i* + 1, *m* + 2, etc., on the rests ("prepare"). The two movements will thus be bound together by *one* shared playing impulse.

[2] Complete the stroke ("play") and release the *i* or *m* resting on the G string for its next plant. The release will also trigger the synchronized movement impulses in step [1] for the *next* note.

[3] In ascending, leave down each left-hand finger so they'll be in place for the descending part of the scale.

[4] In descending, simply *release* each left-hand finger exactly as *m* or *i* plants on the rests ("prepare") and then play the new note, which is already in place. Continue to the end and repeat.

TIP: The rhythmic feel of this process and the sense of constant physical contact with the strings can be compared with swinging hand to hand on a playground overhead ladder or even pedaling a bicycle.

DYNAMIC STROKE PREPARATION IN ARPEGGIOS

To consolidate your command of dynamic right-hand preparations, we'll use some more of Mauro Giuliani's *120 Daily Exercises for the Right Hand*, introduced in Book Two, pages 6–7.

Simultaneous Preparation (The "Full Plant")

As symbolized by the vertical bracket in the music example here, plant for the basic *p-i-m-a* arpeggio just as you would for a **block chord**. Then play each finger in turn and repeat the cycle. **Simultaneous planting**, also known as "block planting," is used for ascending arpeggios and the ascending notes in complex arpeggios.

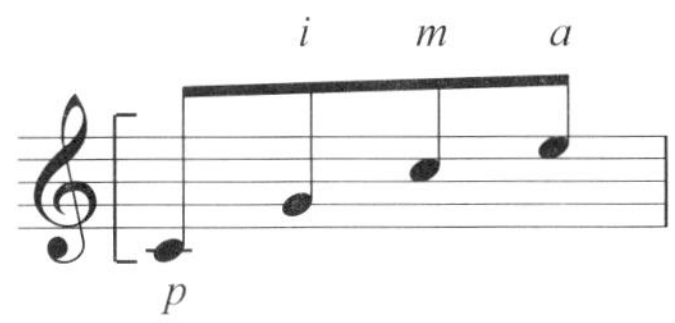

TIP: Oftentimes, students will unconsciously release the planted position of *a* when *m* plays, or even both *m* and *a* when *i* plays. Since you'll lose the benefit of dynamic preparation whenever that happens, be sure to keep *m* and *a* well-planted until they have to play.

Practice the basic *p-i-m-a* exercise below very slowly, synchronizing your hands properly on the chord changes from C to G7 and back. By damping the strings, planting ensures that chord changes will be smooth and relaxed, with no unwanted string noise.

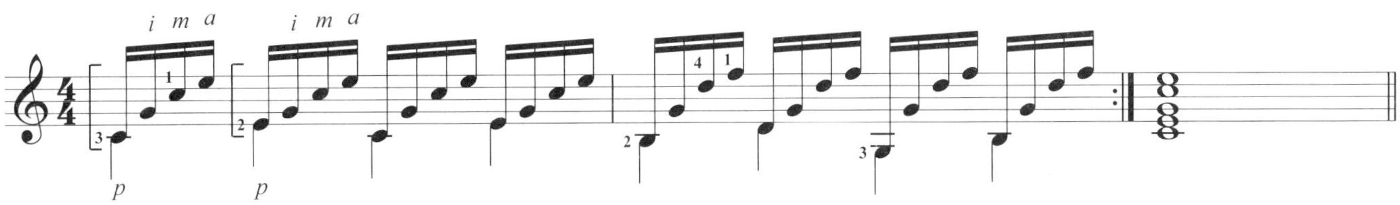

Consecutive Preparations ("Sequential Planting")

The secret of dynamic preparation for descending arpeggios is to plant your fingers consecutively by overlapping each *execution* with the next *preparation* impulse. When done carefully, the seamless connection between neuromuscular impulses will make your fingers feel like they're *chained* together. Usually called "sequential planting," the technique is symbolized here by the horizontal brackets which link consecutive notes in this basic *p-a-m-i* arpeggio:

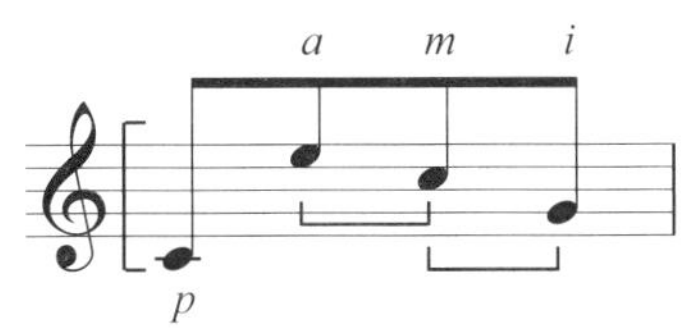

Use the following four-step approach to practice the *p-a-m-i* exercise below:

[1] Plant *p* and *a* simultaneously on C and E, and play the C.

[2] As you play the E with *a*, bring *m* smartly into a planted position on the B string with enough force to seat the nail firmly and take up some slack on the string.

[3] As you play the C with *m*, do the same with *i* for the third string.

[4] As *i* plays the G, complete the cycle by simultaneously planting *p* and *a*.

TIP: When these movements are well-executed, your fingertips will feel like they're actually *sticking* to the strings the way your boots will stick to the ground when walking in mud or snow.

Fine-Tuning Your Preparation Technique with Arpeggios

The following Giuliani exercises will further develop your planting technique with various combinations of ascending and descending preparations. Also, from here on, you *won't* need to simultaneously plant your thumb and the next finger(s) to play, except at the start of an exercise. Once you've begun, it's more efficient to let *p* make its own preparation, triggered by the preceding finger-stroke. *Then*, as *p* plays, its recovery movement (shown on p. 6) will sympathetically pull the next *finger(s)* to play into the correct planted position. Synchronizing your thumb and finger preparations this way will generate a dynamic rotary cycle like that of a waterwheel.

We'll revisit the concept of dynamic preparation in the sections devoted to other essential left- and right-hand techniques, but now it's time to move on to some music and new music concepts!

3/8 Time and Thirty-Second Notes

Just like 6/8 time, in **3/8** time, eighth notes get one beat and sixteenth notes get a *half* beat. **Thirty-second notes** divide a beat into *fourths*, as shown:

Count music in 3/8 as indicated below. In bars 5 and 6, notice that you count dotted sixteenth/thirty-second notes just like dotted eighth/sixteenths in 3/4 or 4/4.

In Aguado's etude below, dotted sixteenth/thirty-second note figures are used as a rhythmic ***motive**. Note also the composer's use of third-beat *rests* as phrase endings. To play these musical silences, just plant for the next chord while simultaneously relaxing your left-hand finger pressure. Since this is an almost intuitive damping technique, with just a bit of practice it will feel entirely natural.

Estudio

Dionisio Aguado
(1784–1849)

Andantino M.M. ♪ = 108

***TIP:** Motives are short musical ideas whose repetition in a piece helps to unify it.

Barred Chords

In this section, we'll start with a brief practical review of partial barring (introduced in Book Two) with a couple of enjoyable etudes, and then tackle the more difficult full barre. As explained in Book Two, barres are identified by the letter C (for Spanish *ceja*, "bar"), plus the fret number. In this book, the *type* of barre is indicated by the fret number (in Roman numerals) preceded by fractions for the number of strings covered. Thus, for a *2nd*-fret barre, the possibilities are: 1/3CII (*two* strings), 1/2CII (*three* strings), 2/3CII (*four*), 5/6CII (*five*), and CII (*all six*).

Barred Chord Etude 1

Charles Duncan

Barred Chord Etude 2

Charles Duncan

THE FULL BARRE

The easiest way to learn the full barre is to start with the fingerings for the Am and E chords shown to the right. With the barred first finger in place of the nut, these movable chord grips can be played up to the 10th fret. Practice changing them back and forth, and be sure to keep your fingers joined together on the changes!

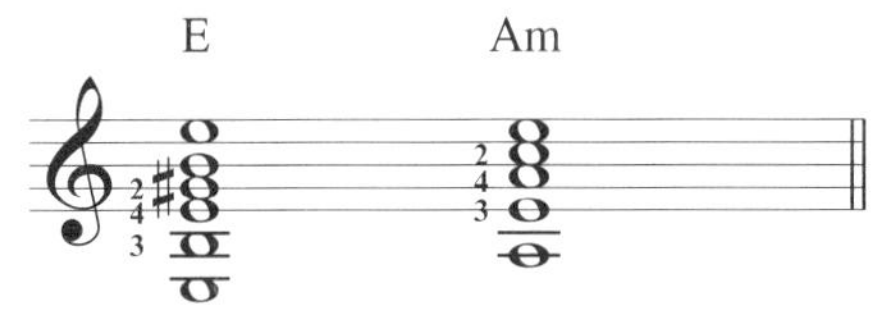

Barred at the 1st fret, they become the F and B♭m chords shown below. Practice as follows:

[1] Make the re-fingered E chord; *then* slide it up a fret and clamp down the barre at the 1st fret.

[2] Strum the F chord in the first photograph and change to the B♭m shown in the second.

[3] Keep your fingers joined on the change, place them simultaneously, and strum the B♭m.

[4] Finally, practice changing the chords back and forth *without* lifting the barre.

TIP: In five- and six-string barres, the leverage comes mainly from the *knuckle* joint. Therefore, you'll need to keep the finger rigid from knuckle to tip with no "give" in the tip-joint or middle joint.

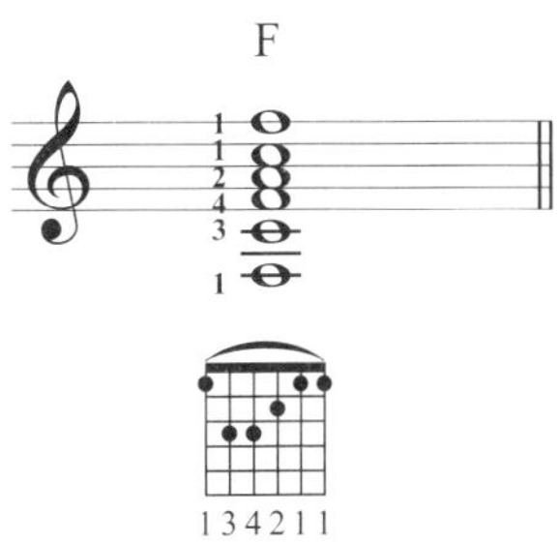

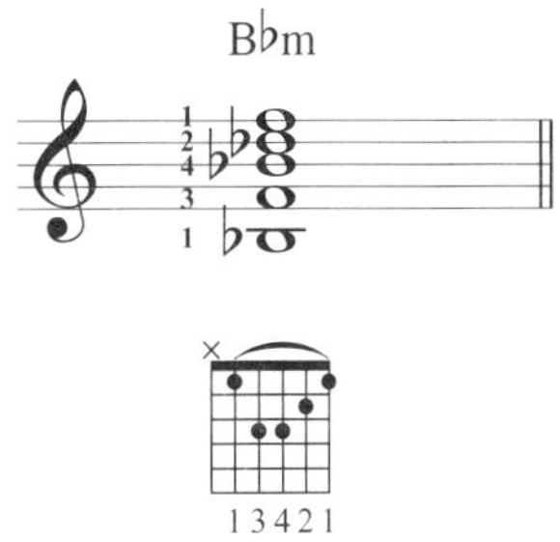

Refining Your Grip for Best Leverage

Students often press too hard with the thumb and try to keep the first finger unnaturally straight. These common errors strain the muscles and waste effort by not providing efficient leverage. You can avoid them by observing the following fine points:

[1] Pressure from the ball of the thumb provides only part of the force needed for a good grip. Most of it comes from **(a)** the adductor and interosseous muscles *between* the thumb and forefinger, and **(b)** the arms, by pulling back slightly against the counterforce from the chest. A tendency to pull back a bit is perfectly normal anyway; just experiment with it until you can feel the leverage relieving the strain on your hand and stop there. With practice, the muscles between your thumb and first finger will get bigger and your barred chord playing will become easier.

[2] Look closely at the photographs, and notice how the first finger presses slightly on its outside edge, rather than completely flat. At the lower frets, this small outward rotation of the finger is natural, and increases its leverage. As you move up the fingerboard, the finger will naturally flatten out, and the extra leverage will come from the better alignment of the hand and upper arm at the higher frets.

The Key of F Major

Since keys with *more* than one flat don't use many open-string fingerings and rely mainly on barred chords, there's not much classical guitar music in those keys. However, with only one flat (B♭), the key of F has some, and its relative minor (Dm) is a commonly used key.*

[1] Memorize the two-octave first-position F scale and practice with staccato articulations. Use the *a-m* as well as the *m-i* fingering to strengthen *a* and improve its independence from *m*. For most players, the *a* finger requires considerable extra work to develop its playing potential.

[2] Memorize and practice the following F major *cadence* slowly, combining GDM (p. 4) with conscious planting to synchronize the hands (p. 8). Formal cadences consist of a short sequence of the primary chords that define any given key—the tonic (I), subdominant (IV), and dominant or dominant seventh (V or V7). The chords are usually in root position, except for the tonic 6/4 chord (tonic over the fifth scale tone) that sometimes precedes the V7 chord as it does here.

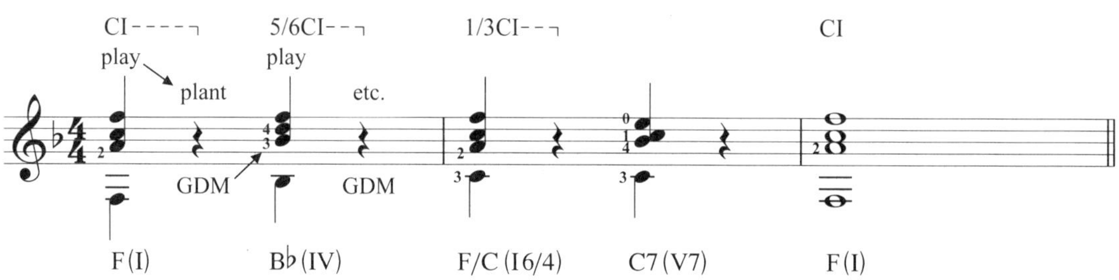

[3] Practice the following scale *pattern* exercise built on the ascending F scale. Pattern exercises provide an enjoyable form of scale practice with benefits such as enhanced fingerboard IQ, left-hand agility, and right-hand scale speed. Don't neglect to practice also with *a-m*!

***TIP:** For good examples in both F and Dm, see the author's *A Modern Approach to Classical Guitar Repertoire, Part One*. For examples of pieces in the much less-used key of B♭ (two flats), see Fernando Sor's famous "Etude 19" in *Twenty Studies for Classical Guitar*, ed. Andrés Segovia (Hal Leonard), and the author's etude "Reverie" in *A Modern Approach to Classical Guitar Repertoire, Part Two.*

Carulli's light-hearted etude below provides an opportunity to use articulations for musical effect by dramatizing the repeated rhythmic motive introduced in measure 1:
(1) Play the eighth-note chords on beats 3 and 6 *forte* and cut them off quickly by planting.
(2) Then, play the already-planted quarter-note chords on beats 1 and 4 somewhat softer and hold them for full time value. When well-learned and played with less effort to create contrast, the effect will be a colorful, interesting, *legato* melodic line.

TIP: The visual symbols for staccato and legato notes are dots and dashes, just like Morse code ("dit-*dah*," etc.). Look for them in the first line as a guide to phrasing for the whole piece.

Etude in F

Ferdinando Carulli
(1770–1841)

The Key of D Minor

[1] Memorize and practice the extended one-octave Dm scales in **(a)** open position, and **(b)** second and third positions. As explained in Book Two, the melodic minor is the form preferred for scales.

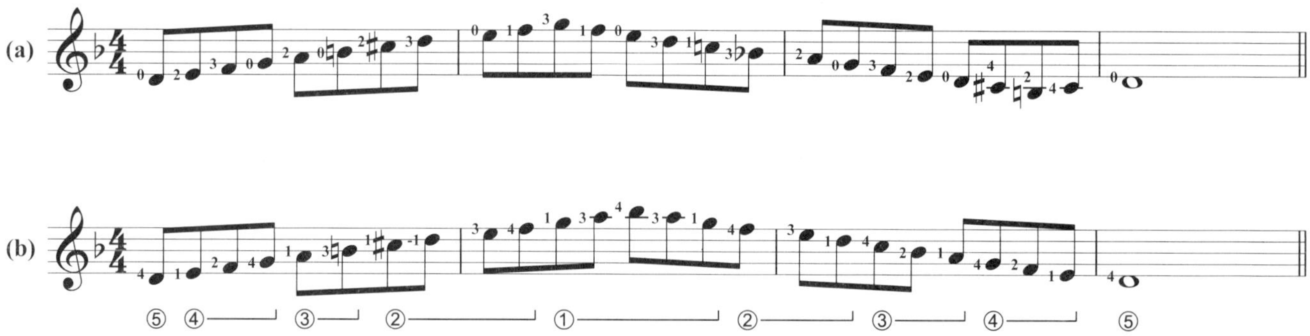

[2] Memorize and practice these Dm cadences using both GDM and conscious synchronization.

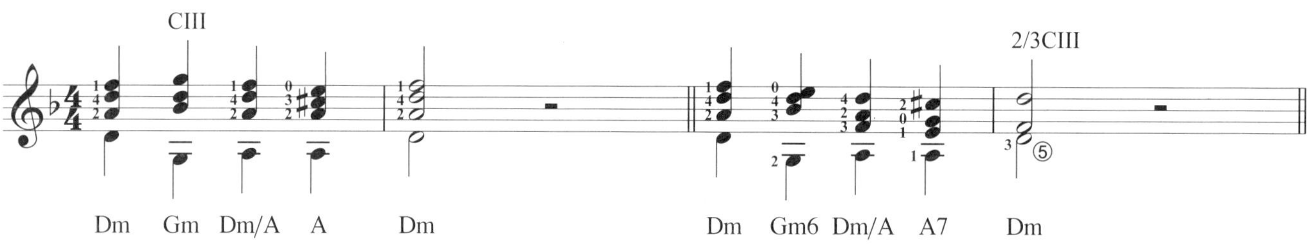

The charming "Minuet" below is a harpsichord piece by England's finest composer of the early Baroque period (the late 17th century). A popular dance form that emerged during Purcell's times, the *minuet* was used both for instrumental solos and as a movement in extended works.

Minuet

Henry Purcell
(1659–1695)

TIP: The fingering in measure 1 is called a *campanelas* fingering (Spanish, "little bells") because of the shimmering resonance created by the overlapped tones. Here, and like the similar fingerings in the last line, it captures the transparent sonority of the harpsichord better than a standard fingering.

USING REST STROKES WITH THE THUMB

Free strokes with *p* are the norm for most playing, but rest strokes are often used for various purposes. To cultivate the technique, practice the lower octave of the F major scale as follows:

[**1**] Plant *p-i-m-a* with the thumb tucked in and the nail firmly seated, as shown on page 5.

[**2**] Push down and in from the thumb's basal segment, with supplementary pressure from the mid-joint and tip-joint to control the stroke. Bring the tip to rest on the fifth string.

[**3**] Recover and plant for the next note with the natural, efficient movement illustrated on page 6.

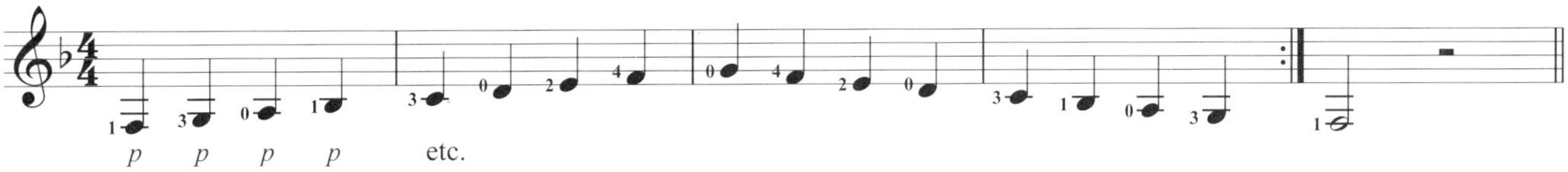

Gaspar Sanz, the premier guitarist of 17th-century Spain, was the author of the first published guitar method (1674), and the *pavana* was a favorite dance of the aristocracy. In the first measure, try using rest strokes with *p* to bring out the dramatic quality of the descending bass line.

Pavana

Gaspar Sanz
(1640–1710)

The Fifth Position

Book Two covered position playing in the second and third positions. In this book, we'll explore the upper fingerboard—an intimidating "twilight zone" if you visualize it as just a *longitudinal* array of notes up to the 12th fret or higher. In contrast, the dynamically prepared approach to reading and playing above the 4th fret is based on secure knowledge of three overlapping, *lateral*, home-base positions—the fifth, seventh, and ninth. The twelfth position can be saved for after you've mastered these interlocked four-fret grids on the free fingerboard.

The fifth-position notes on the first string, as shown to the right, are A (5th fret), A♯/B♭ (6th fret), B (7th fret), and C (8th fret). Notes on the other five strings are the same as in first position, but now they are found on the next lower string as shown below for the 2nd- and 3rd-fret notes.

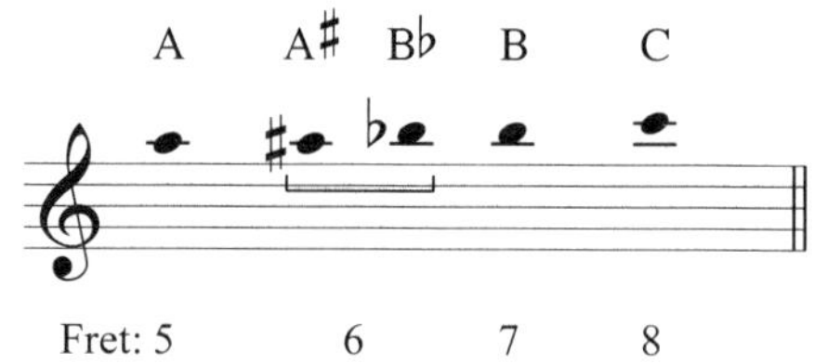

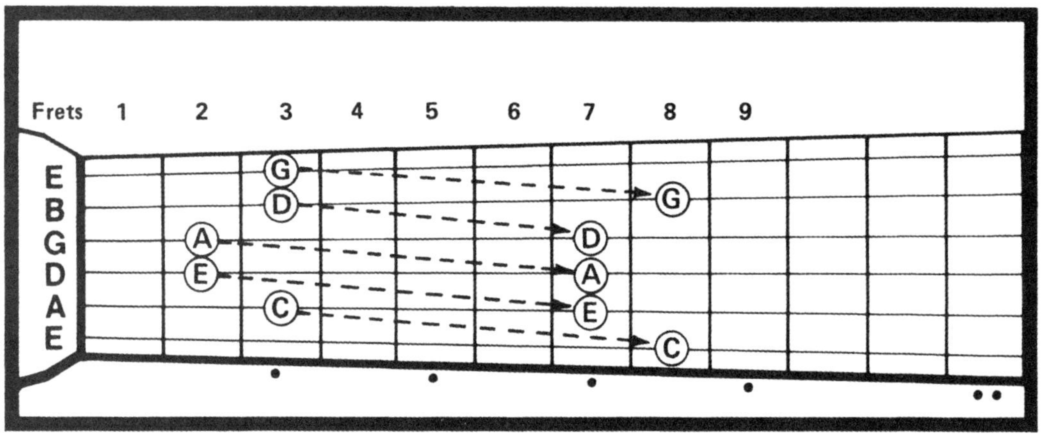

TIP: Remember the "rule of five"—first-position notes are located *five* frets higher on the next lower string, with one exception. Because of how the guitar is tuned, first-position *B-string* notes are *four* frets higher on the G string. For ready reference, the chart below shows *all* the notes in fifth position.

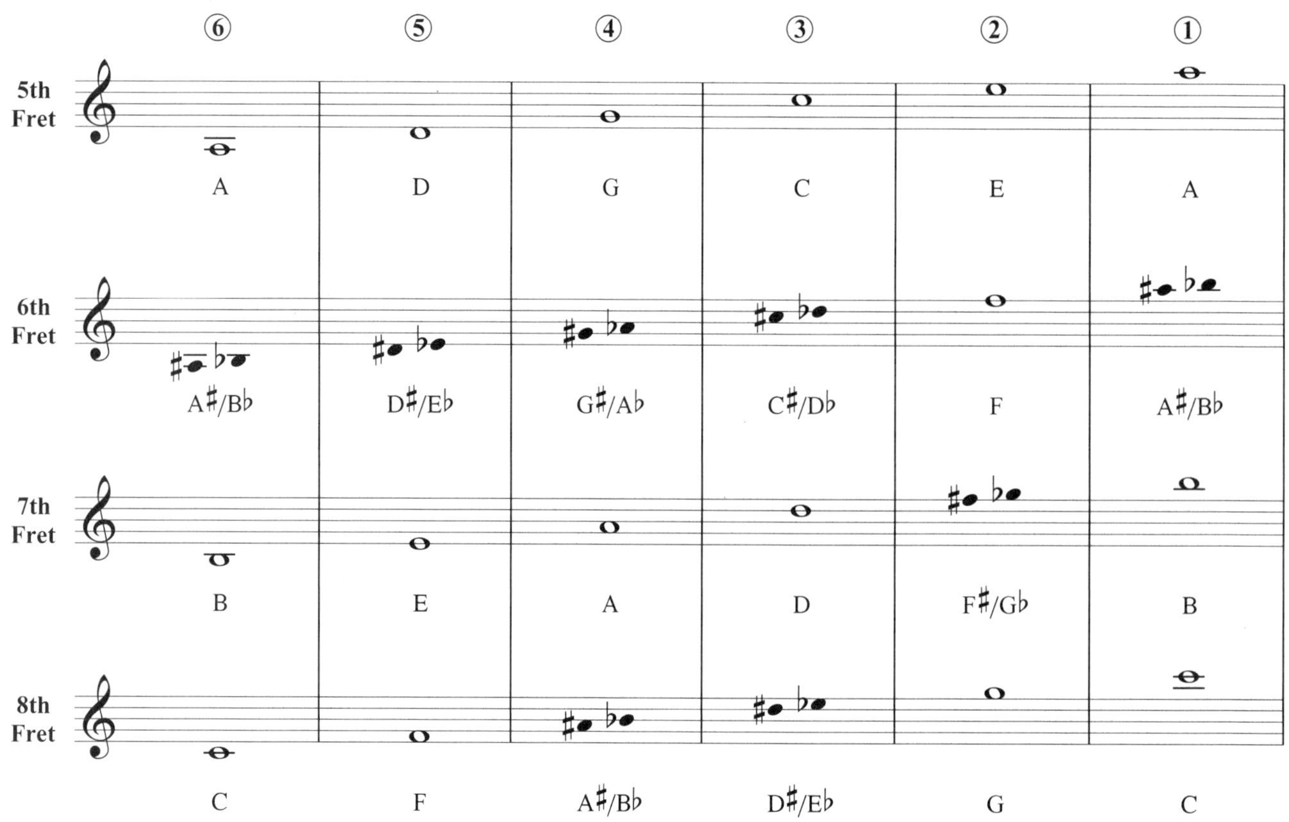

FIFTH-POSITION SCALE PATTERN STUDIES

Since they're based on logical sequences of scale motives, pattern studies are great for learning the lateral note-grids of the upper fingerboard. Practice the patterns below with the fingers curved and spaced as shown on page 5, and *without* letting them uncurl when they lift. Instead, your fingers should pivot from the knuckle only so that they won't have to flex inward on the return. Correct finger movements are simply up and down, like the pistons in automobile engines.

TIP: In the right-hand fingering, note the reversal of *m* and *i* which occurs at the midpoint of each study. By making this simple change of sequence, you'll avoid awkward **cross-fingerings** on the descending string changes (i.e., where *m* rather than *i* would have to play the lower string).

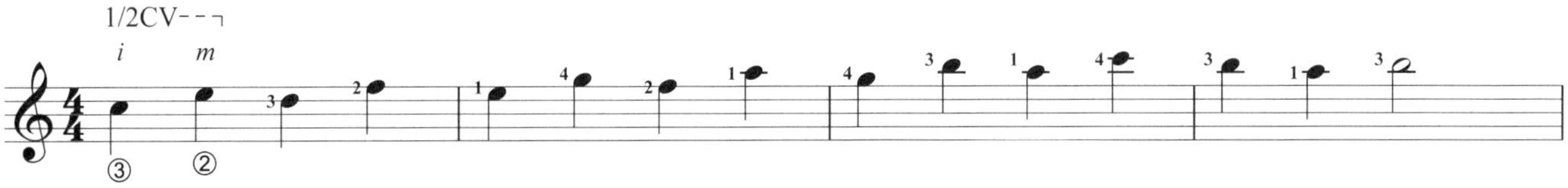

The Pivot Shift

Position playing sometimes requires a one-fret excursion to the next lower or higher fingerboard position. Since the distance to be covered is so small, usually you can just leave the thumb fixed as the pivot for a hand movement that doesn't involve the whole arm. In such cases, you make the shift either by **(a)** a finger-slide, or **(b)** a contraction from the wrist, as indicated in the Am and G scale patterns below. Practice both until these economical shift movements feel natural.

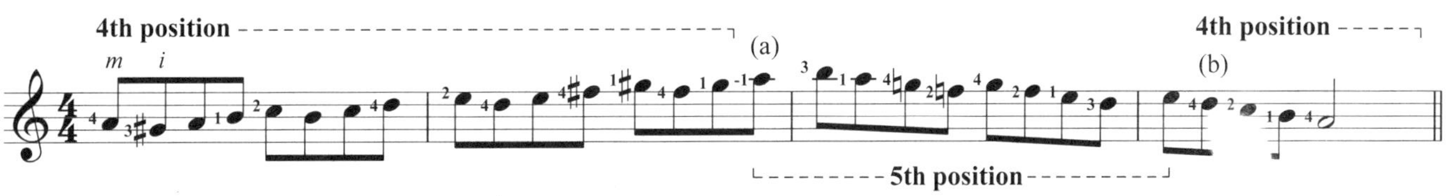

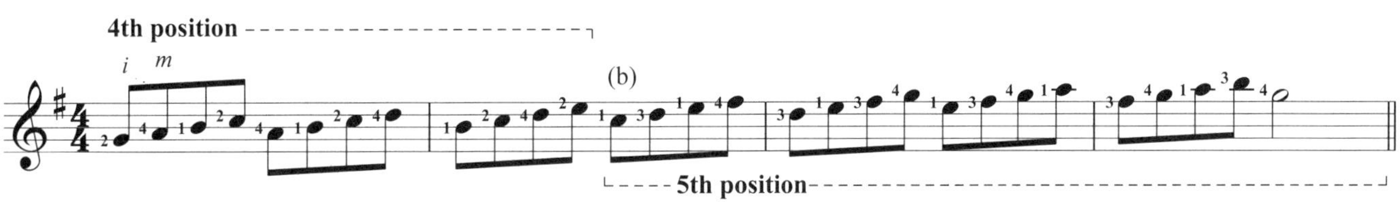

The two-octave C scale below provides a logical model of the fifth-position note layout that will help orient you to the position as a secure home base. Memorize and practice it with extra attention to the *fourth-finger extension* used for B on string 4. Like pivot shifts, such extensions are also used in position playing from time to time. Be sure to keep your first finger anchored on the fourth-string G to maintain the stability of the position as you reach for the B.

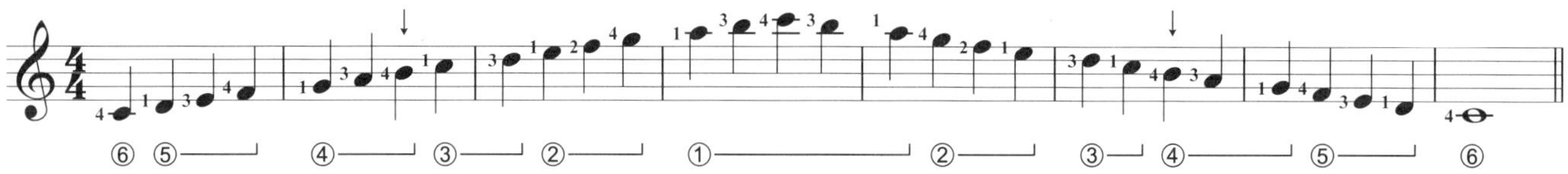

TIP: The melody of "Joy to the World" is based entirely on the higher octave of the above scale.

Joy to the World

G.F. Handel
(1685–1759)

Allegro M.M. ♩ = 76

With different lyrics, this romantic gondolier's song from 19th-century Naples is well-known as a traditional Yuletide carol, especially in Scandinavia. Although it's based in the fifth position, note the fourth-finger extension in measure 6, which in *this* case pulls the hand into sixth position for just a moment. In the next measure, you'll return to fifth position with a small pivot shift from the wrist (type b). In measures 11–15, pivot shifts that also include the finger-slide (type a) provide a smooth, comfortable fingering while retaining the security of the home base.

Santa Lucia

Traditional Italian Song

Moderato M.M. ♩ = 84

Dynamically Prepared, Goal-Directed Shifts

Unlike pivot shifts, changes of fingerboard position require movement of the *whole arm*. Since the weight of the arm and the inertial forces involved are significant factors, that's a problem in itself. When coupled with a lack of mental anticipation, chances are that the shift will be hurried, jerky, and stressful. In contrast, good shift technique is fluid, graceful, and stress-free. But how?

Guide fingers will always help, but the secret of effortless shifting is another form of dynamic preparation and goal-directed movement (GDM). First, *visualize* the new fingerboard formation as clearly as a chord diagram. Then, rather than move the whole arm as a fixed unit, *divide* its movement like a baseball pitch into a beginning, middle, and end. The movements for ascending and descending shifts will be different, but in both the elbow is the point of control. Its movement precedes the hand's, and the resulting inertial forces propel the hand effortlessly toward the new position.

The illustrations below will give you an idea of the arm, elbow, and hand movements needed for ascending and descending shifts. Practice both types in "super slo-mo," as follows:

[**1**] For shifts to a *higher* position, [**a**] start with a little backswing of your elbow that sets it in clockwise motion. At that point, moving inertia will take over, and [**b**] as the elbow adducts toward the body, [**c**] transport the hand easily to its destination. The result is a shift that feels as if your hand is floating into its new position.

[**2**] For shifts to a *lower* position, [**a**] start by abducting your elbow away from the body to a point beneath the new fingerboard position. Then, with the elbow as a pivot for the forearm's pendular movement, [**b**] use a *counter*-clockwise upper-arm rotation that will [**c**] "float" your hand into the new position while [**d**] the elbow falls naturally back toward the body.

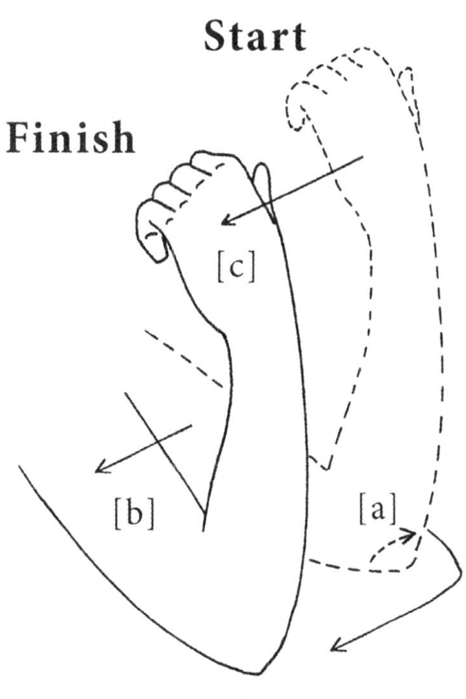

(1) Ascending

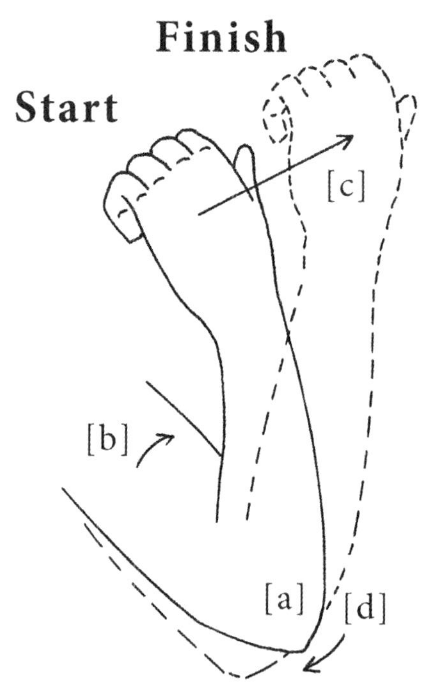

(2) Descending

✔ **TIP:** Remember that the elbow *always initiates the movement*. In ascending, it describes a small clockwise semicircle that generates enough momentum to get your hand to the target fret with no further effort. In descending, it achieves the same objective by torquing the hand in the *opposite* direction with a gentle see-saw movement of the forearm. For both types, your eyes should *lead* the hand. Don't fall into the trap of just *tracking* the hand's movement with your eyes!

CHORD AND SCALE SHIFTS

Use the following approach to memorize and practice the two cadences in F. Take your time on the shifts, making sure to *lead* the hand with your eyes. Once you've mastered the proper movement forms, the brain's motor areas will take over and transform them into graceful, reliable reflexes.

[1] Plant after each chord, look toward the target fret, and visualize the new chord.

[2] For *ascending* shifts, start the backswing with your elbow; for *descending* shifts, move the elbow away from the body and toward a point beneath the new fingerboard position.

[3] In ascending, "float" the hand to its new position by completing the elbow's outward rotation. In descending, use leverage from the elbow's adduction back toward the body for the same purpose.

[4] Carefully shape your fingers into the new chord form as you approach the target position.

[5] Press down the fingers and play the chord.

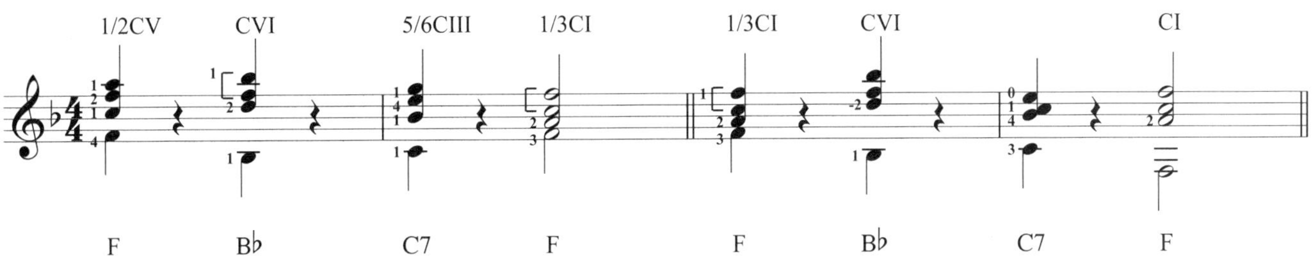

Practice the following C and F scales likewise, while noting the differences from chord shifts:

[1] Since only one string is involved, the shift is simpler and requires somewhat less energy.

[2] The *first* finger serves as a guide to the fifth position in each case. As indicated by the dotted-line brackets, *leave it down* as an anchor to stabilize the position until it's needed to play again.

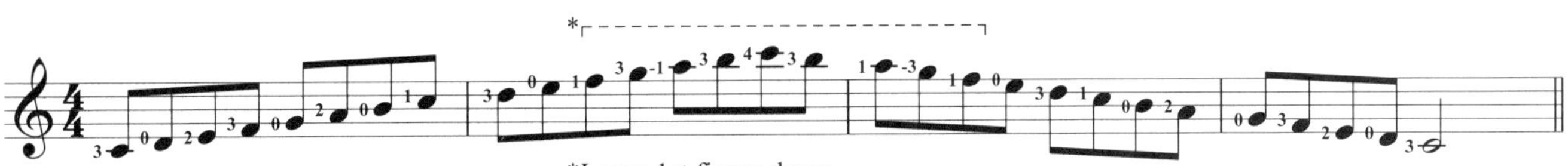

*Leave 1st finger down.

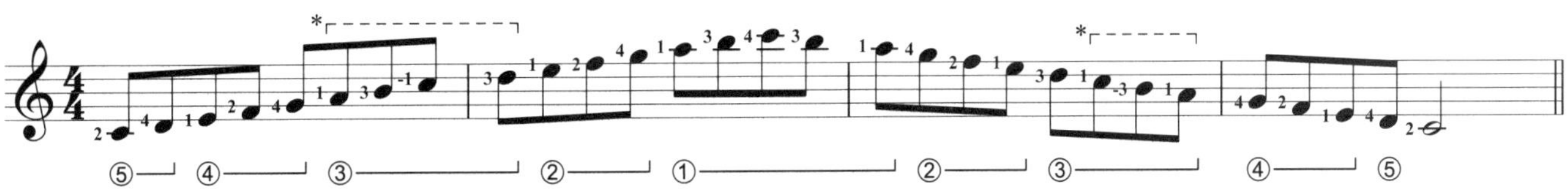

*Leave 1st finger down.

PRACTICING ARPEGGIATED PIECES WITH BLOCK CHORDS

As for most arpeggiated pieces, practicing the charming study by Francisco Tárrega on the next page in the form of *block chords*, as shown below, will shortcut your mastery of it. This particular use of dynamic preparation will enable you to hear and see the underlying chord structure, sharpen your visualization of how it lies on the fingerboard, and concentrate on your left hand's goal-directed movement forms. When coupled with aggressive planting to perfect the synchronization of your hands, your technical command of the piece will be secure. Then, when practicing it as written, you can focus on bringing out the melody with the *a* finger's heavy down-and-in push into the string, called a *half*-rest stroke (see Book Two, p. 18). Where added melodic emphasis is called for, use *full* rest strokes as indicated by the accent marks (>).

Using the Tip-Joint Hinge Barre

This piece will also introduce you to the tip-joint **hinge barre**, an easy technique used intuitively by good players when needed. In measures 10 and 14, simply flatten your index finger's tip-segment to grab the F on beat 3—*while still holding the C*—by collapsing the arch of your tip-joint. Then, on the fourth beat, "hinge" back up onto your tip to play the open string E, while *still* holding the C.

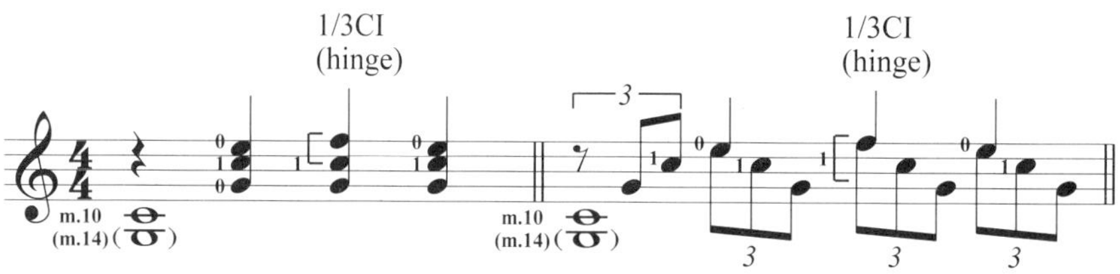

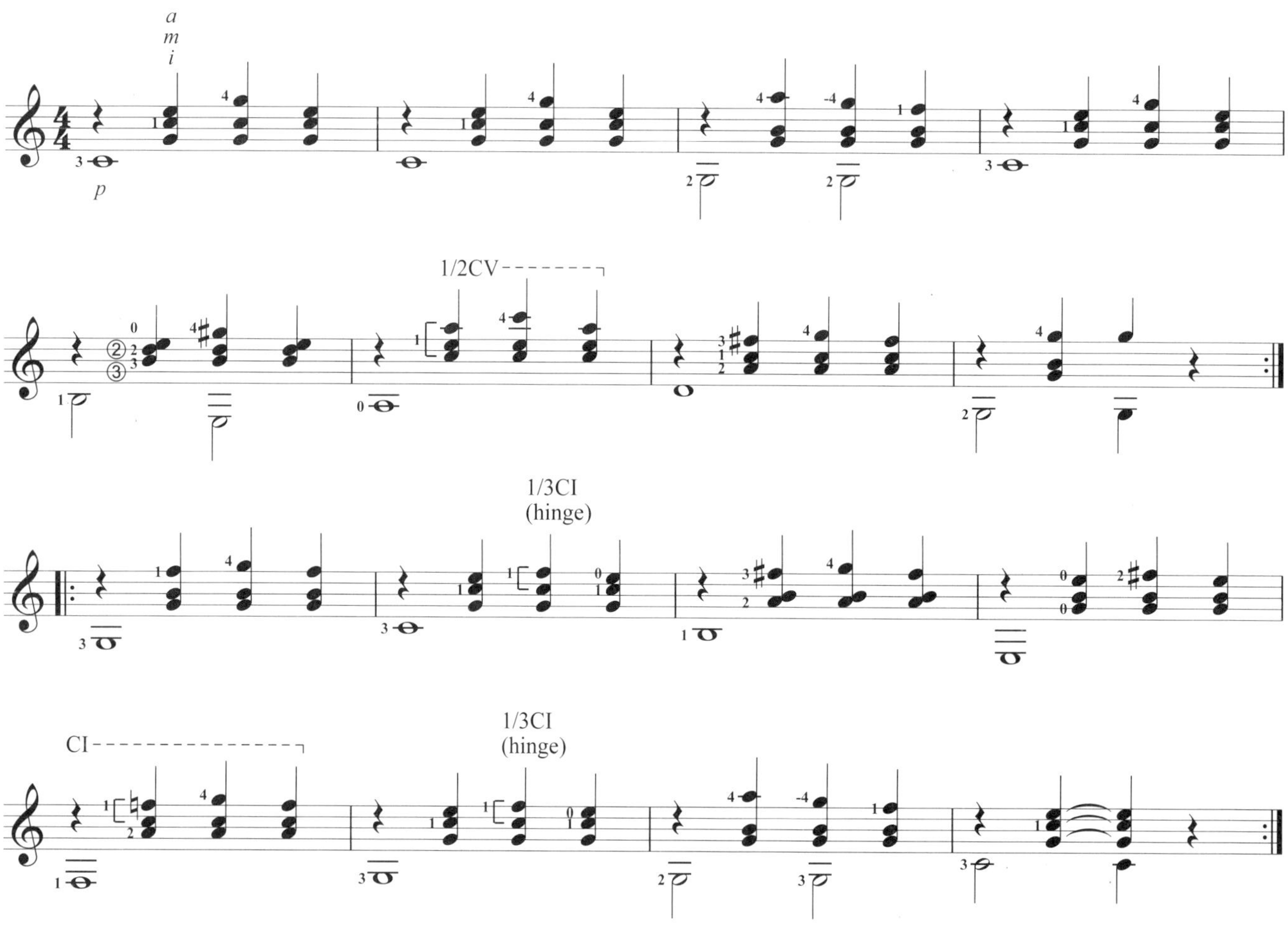

Study No. 1

Francisco Tárrega
(1852–1909)

Andante M.M. ♩ = 80

The following "Leccion" (Spanish, "lesson") by Sor provides an excellent practice model for stress-free shifting, with the tips shown below the piece as a working guide—they're keyed to the numbers you'll see over several measures. The *alla breve* time signature (₵), known as "cut time," means that the count is based on the *half* note—*two* relaxed beats to the measure instead of a frantic four.

Leccion in Am

Fernando Sor
(1778–1839)

Moderato M.M. 𝅗𝅥 = 52

[1] Use a regular descending shift (not a pivot shift) to reach the G♯.

[2] Note how naturally the out-and-in elbow movement transports the hand to the first position, while the open E masks the shift.

[3] Plant *p* on the A string as you dynamically prepare the shift back to fifth position with a little backswing of the elbow.

[4] Note how easily the clockwise elbow rotation propels the hand back to the 5th fret.

[5] Here, the out-and-in elbow movement torques the first finger into position on the 3rd fret without stress, while the *campanelas* fingering at the end of the measure masks the shift.

[6] Observe the dynamics indicated and hold the climax chords for slightly more than full value.

[7] The musical climax here is challenging, but the shifts are all facilitated by a guide finger, including the first. (Note how it glided silently up to fifth position.)

Carulli's dramatic D minor prelude also provides a great opportunity to prove the benefits of practicing arpeggio pieces minus the arpeggiation. When you can sight-read it fluently, practice in the form of *p-i-m* block chords while concentrating on the left hand's goal-directed movements and the right hand's extra-firm preparations before position shifts.

Prelude in Dm

Ferdinando Carulli
(1770–1841)

The following composition by the author is in the Romantic style made famous by early 19th-century piano composers such as Beethoven, Schubert, Schumann, and Mendelssohn. The melody should be emphasized with the deliberately solid half-rest stroke. At the points of extra melodic significance indicated by the accent marks, a full rest stroke would be best.

Remembrance

Charles Duncan

The author's "Song Without Words," also in the 19th-century Romantic style, recalls some of Felix Mendelssohn's beautiful "Songs Without Words"—a series of short, lyrical piano solos which have long been favorites in the piano repertoire. The piece also provides various opportunities to practice your goal-directed, dynamically prepared shift technique in an interesting form.

Song Without Words

Charles Duncan

Andante con moto M.M. ♩. = 56

Dynamic Slurring

Like position shifting, dynamic slur technique includes the sympathetic participation of muscles from the wrist to the shoulder. Rigid hand and arm positions therefore should be avoided, and the palm of your hand should stay close to the edge of fingerboard so the wrist can remain straight (see again on p. 5). When slurring on the lowest strings, let your palm touch the edge of the fingerboard.

ASCENDING ("HAMMERING ON")

[1] Curve and space your fingers as illustrated on page 5, so their tips point straight down.

[2] Use "Micro-GDM" to aim their attack at a spot right behind the metal fret, where the purchase on the string is best and a clean slur is therefore the easiest. Try for a sharp, percussive impact that you can actually *hear* as a crisp note articulation.

[3] Use the muscles in the heel of your hand, pivoting from the wrist, to support the finger-attack. Especially when hammering on with the fourth finger, you should feel those muscles contract into a power-source for the movement. Some rotary play of the forearm, pivoting from the elbow, will also help maximize the force transmitted to your fingertips.

[4] Avoid the common pitfall of pivoting the fingers from the knuckle only. Dynamic ascending slurs are powered also by energy from the wrist, elbow, and shoulder.

DESCENDING ("PULLING OFF")

[1] Curve and space your fingers the same way, with the tips right behind the metal frets.

[2] The correct finger action is a lateral flex of the tip which actually *plucks* the string. A common error is weak tip-joint flexion—a goal-directed pull-off is aimed straight into the palm.

[3] Since this motion can *also* sound the next higher string inadvertently when slurring on any string but the first, play these slurs as *left-hand rest strokes.* Aim your fingertip straight back so that it bumps into the next higher string and recoils back up into the dynamically prepared attack position.

[4] As with ascending slurs, sympathetic participation of the arm and wrist should be encouraged, not inhibited. Some energetic contraction of the heel of the hand from the wrist, supported by a bit of forearm rotation, will multiply the force available at the fingertip and spare the fingers from having to do all the work.

The exercises on the next page combine ascending and descending slurs in various ways. As shown for Ex. 1, play as far as seventh position by shifting up one fret at a time, and descend the same way. Practice them on all six strings with your metronome, listening for an even division of the beat. To offset the common tendency to rush slurs, practice *also* by dotting the rhythm as shown in the warm-up exercise at the top of the page. This counterintuitive but extremely effective practice technique will retard the slurs and gradually instill the ability to control their timing more accurately.

For Ex. 6, 7, and 8, use this comparable eighth + two sixteenths rhythmic formula to develop control and keep the triplets from galloping:

Warm-Up Ex.

Ex. 1

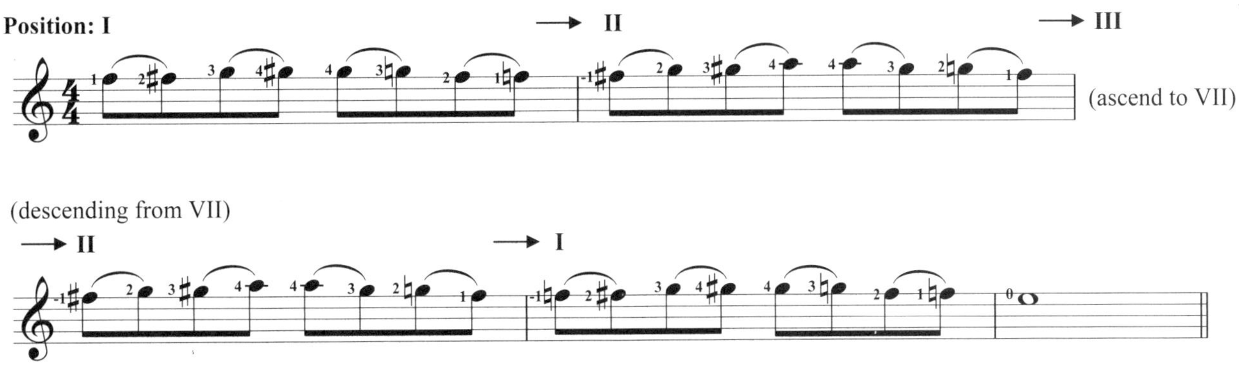

Ex. 2

Ex. 3

Ex. 4

Ex. 5

Ex. 6

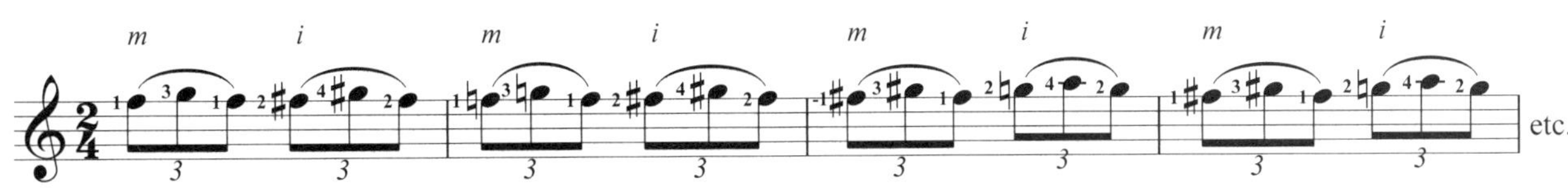

Ex. 7

Ex. 8

The Key of D Major

The key of D and its relative, B minor, use F# and C# in their key signatures. Both keys are commonly used in classical guitar music, particularly D major. To begin, memorize and practice the extended one-octave D major scales in second and fourth position:

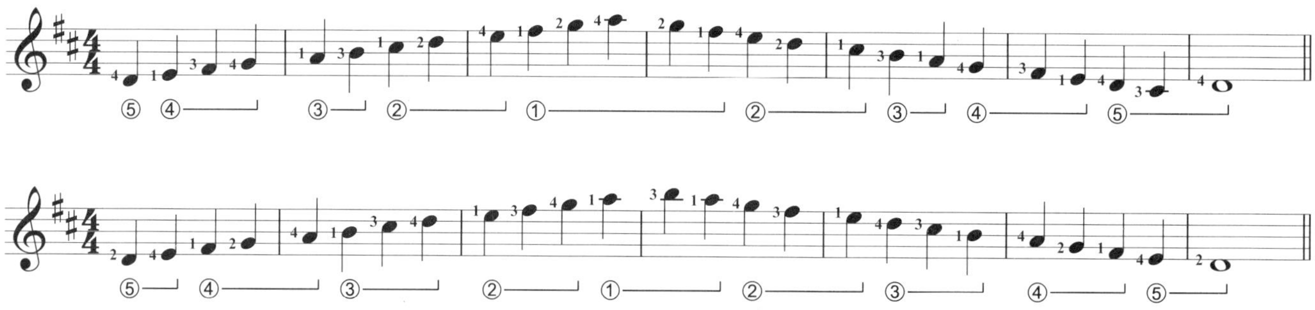

Memorize and practice these D major cadences for clean articulation and synchronization of the hands. Then practice in the broken chord forms which follow them, using precise consecutive preparation technique: play *p*-plant *i*, play *i*-plant *a/m*, play *a/m*-plant *i*, play *i*-plant *p*, etc. Remember the importance of feeling that your fingers are chained together! (See again p. 9.)

In the following scale pattern study, the alternation between fourth and fifth position is made easy by keeping the thumb fixed and using pivot shifts. Note also the right-hand fingering—until the final measure, there are only three cross-fingerings (see the arrows). If the one that would occur in the last measure seems too awkward, you can *drag* your *i* finger through a double rest-stroke as shown. Although not often taught, the "drag-stroke" with *i* is used by many top players.

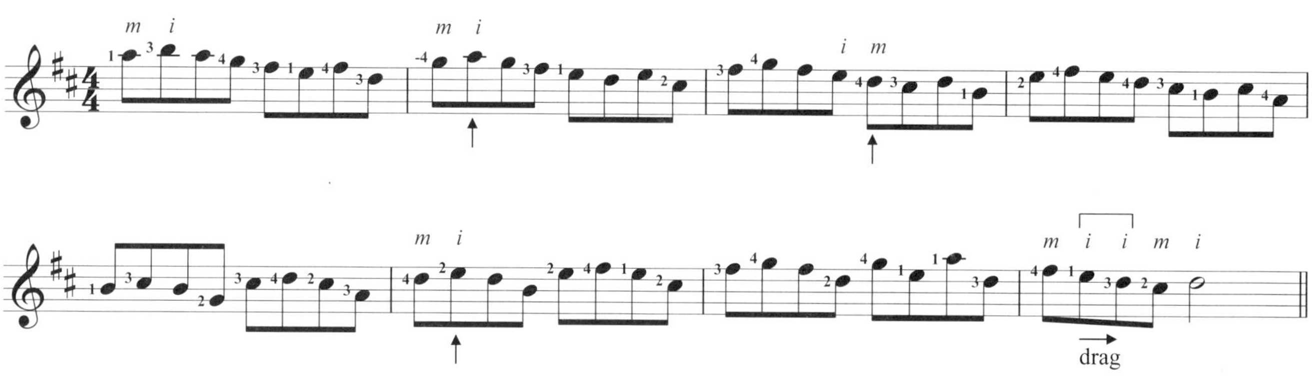

Couperin's "Le Petit Rien" ("The Little Trifle") is a good example of the harpsichord compositions by France's premier early Baroque composer. Frequently, they have whimsical titles that reveal the composer's intentions—here, that the piece is an amusing diversion to be played with a light, sparkling touch. To help create that effect, use the articulations shown in the first measure wherever this important rhythmic-melodic motive occurs.

Le Petit Rien

François Couperin
(1668–1733)

Allegretto M.M. ♩= 120

Anton Diabelli, a prominent Viennese music publisher as well as a prolific composer, authored numerous attractive guitar pieces. This one is in the style of a popular dance form in which lines of couples faced off *opposite* each other—a "*contra*-dance," known in French as *contredanse, kontratanz* in German, and "country dance" in English. It's from one of his many editions of music for the big 19th-century market of European guitar enthusiasts.

Contradance

Anton Diabelli
(1781–1858)

The next piece typifies a fast Renaissance and Baroque dance form in triple meter that was named for its speed, the word for "running" in Italian (*corrente*) and French (*courante*). Not much is known about Carlo Calvi except that he was a prestigious court musician in 17th-century Italy and composed many good pieces for guitar such as this one. (For another, see the author's *A Modern Approach to Classical Guitar Repertoire, Part One.*)

Corrente

Carlo Calvi
(c.1610–1670)

Moderato M.M. 𝅗𝅥. **= 56**

Embellishment: Common Ornaments

Book Two introduced the use of single and double grace notes as melodic ornamentation. We'll revisit them here and then go on to the other most common embellishments.

The grace note is usually the upper neighbor to the one it embellishes and is played with a pull-off. Although written before the beat, it's played *on* the beat simultaneously with any lower tones:

Double grace notes use either the upper *or* lower neighbor to decorate the main tone. If using the lower, this ornament is known as a **mordent** and is played by pulling off and hammering on. If it's the upper neighbor, it's called an **inverted mordent** and is played by hammering on and pulling off.

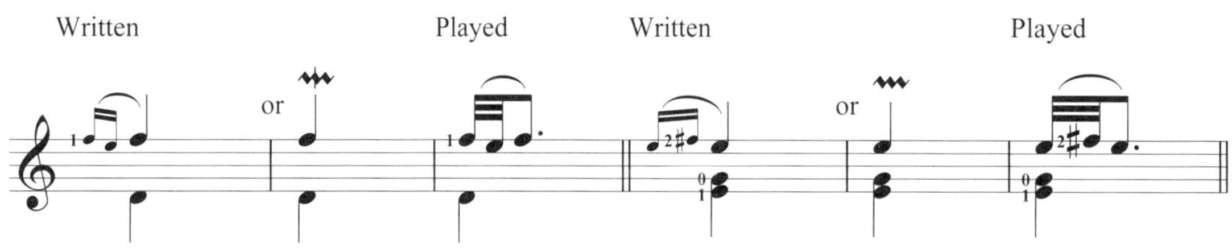

Both types are played simultaneously together with any lower notes, and can be written either in small, cue-sized notes or indicated by signs. For the mordent, the sign resembles a tilde bisected with a stroke symbol (⩫); for the inverted mordent, the stroke is omitted (∼). The mordent was used very frequently in music written before 1800, while the inverted mordent has been a common embellishment since then.

TIP: Just like grace notes, mordents succeed by tricking the ear, which naturally gravitates toward the main tone. Consequently, when well-played, they sound as if the main tone falls *on* the beat, *not* a fraction after it!

In contrast, the **appoggiatura**—an upper or lower neighbor to the main tone—borrows *half* of the main tone's time value, thereby creating a brief dissonance. It can be written out or indicated by a small note *without* the diagonal stroke used for a grace note. The examples below exemplify its usage to decorate cadences: **(1)** is from Bach's "Minuet in G" (from *A Modern Approach to Classical Guitar Repertoire, Part One*); **(2)** is the second ending to de Visée's "Minuet" on page 39.

To these embellishments may be added the **turn**—a group of four notes played as a continuous slur: **(1)** upper neighbor, **(2)** main tone, **(3)** lower neighbor, and **(4)** main tone. Its symbol is a letter "S" on its side, written over the main tone and played as shown in the first measure below. If written *between* that note and the next one, it's played as shown in the second measure. Turns originated in the late 17th century and remained a standard ornament well into the 19th century.

Finally, there's the **trill** (*tr*)—a series of rapid alternations between a main tone and its upper neighbor. The modern trill begins on the main tone, but in music written before 1800, trills usually began on the upper note to create more dissonance with the underlying harmony. The "***tr***" sign is often followed by a wavy line to indicate the trill's duration, and the traditional way to execute trills is with a continuous slur. A more recent innovation is the use of **cross-string trills**, which are especially appropriate in Baroque music—see the Weiss "Sarabande," page 45.

Trills can be used to decorate any note long enough to accommodate them, but their most common use is to dramatize phrase endings. In the first example below, the trill finishes with an eighth note that dynamically anticipates the tonic resolution. In the second, the trill finishes even more dynamically with a turn that anticipates the resolution. As shown in the first example, the number of notes in a trill depends largely on the tempo, and thus, the amount of time available.

Ex. 1

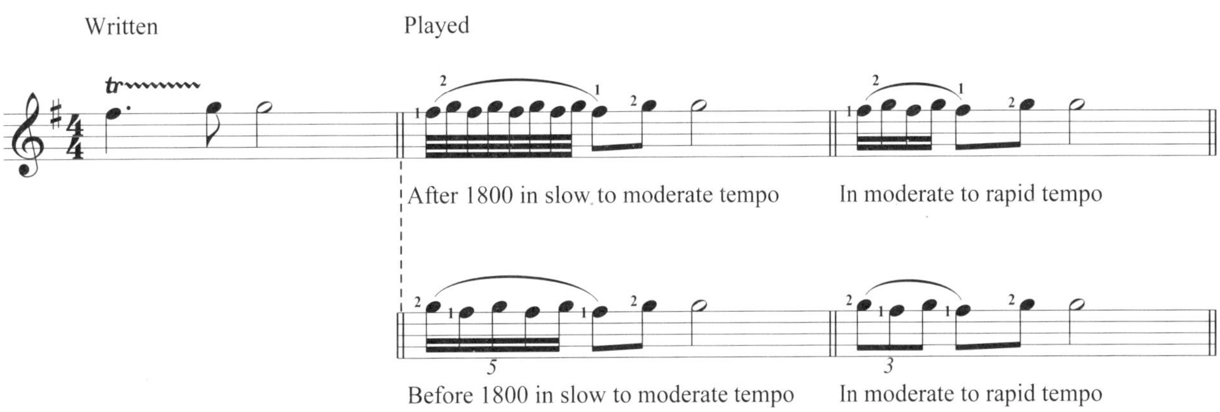

Ex. 2

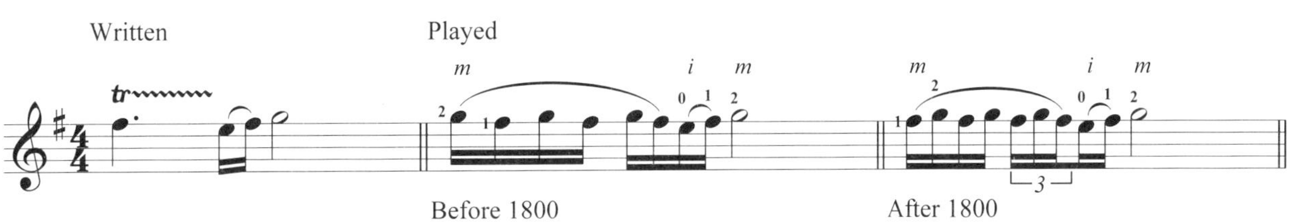

What we've covered provides a foundation for playing music that calls for embellishment, but to pursue the subject further, there are many print and online resources. For example, Frank Koonce's *Johann Sebastian Bach: The Solo Lute Works* (Neil Kjos, 2002) contains a practical overview of Baroque ornamentation, and for cross-string trills, various reliable tutorials are available on YouTube. The best scholarly guide to the subject is Frederick Neumann's *Ornamentation in Baroque and Post-Baroque Music* (Princeton University Press, 1983).

Besides being a fine composition, the piece below is from the first book of printed music for the guitar's immediate ancestor, the Spanish *vihuela—El Maestro* by Luis de Milán (1536). The slow, stately *pavana* (English, *pavan*; French, *pavane*) was a favorite dance form among the Renaissance aristocracies of Europe, which is probably why de Milán included six of them in his book.

TIP: Although this is a challenging piece, the new time signature shouldn't be a problem. It's counted just like 3/4, except that in 3/2 the *half* note gets one beat and *quarter* notes get a *half* beat.

Pavana No. 6

Luis de Milán
(c.1500–1561)

On the next page, the author's piece is a tribute to the great Baroque lutenist Sylvius Leopold Weiss (see p. 45). Written in the style of his dreamy-sounding Preludes, it utilizes *campanelas* fingerings (p. 16) to create the overlapping sonorities of the Baroque lute. In contrast, the "Minuet" by Robert de Visée exemplifies the style of the French five-string Baroque guitar, including the highly ornamented repeat of the last four measures. A popular court musician during the reign of Louis XV, de Visée's compositions are now favorites among contemporary Baroque guitarists.

Prelude in the Style of S.L. Weiss

Charles Duncan

Poco Lento M.M. ♩ = 84

Minuet

Robert de Visée
(1655–1732)

Moderato M.M. ♩ = 120

The Key of B Minor

Although not used so much as its relative major, there's a goodly number of fine classical guitar pieces in the key of Bm. To learn this key, begin with the following two-octave melodic minor scale. On the ascending and descending position shifts, remember to look ahead and lead with the elbow.

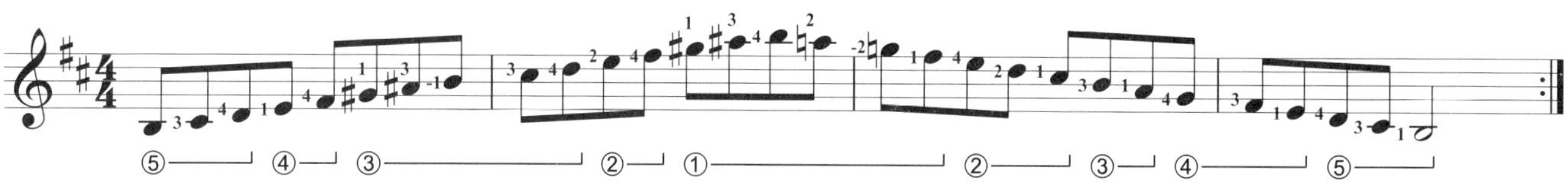

Memorize and practice the following cadence and arpeggio exercise. When playing the arpeggios, concentrate on sequential planting and well-prepared chord changes (see pp. 7–8).

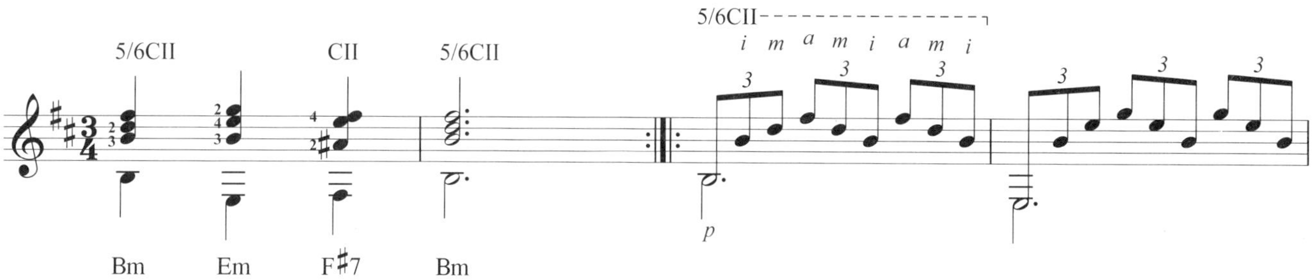

THUMB DEVELOPMENT AND SCALE PLAYING WITH *p-i* ALTERNATION

Because of its natural strength and versatility, the thumb can be a powerful weapon in your arsenal of right-hand technique if you cultivate its capabilities. Besides bass-note emphasis with the rest stroke (p. 17), there are two more techniques it's time for you to learn: **(1)** rest-stroke bass notes in arpeggios for emphasis and right-hand stability, and **(2)** *p-i* alternation to play bass-string scales or scale fragments.

[1] Practice the previous arpeggio exercise with the rest-stroke thumb technique described on p. 17. Leave *p* resting on the next higher string, and synchronize its recovery for the next stroke with the last stroke of the *i* finger in each measure (see again p. 10).

[2] Practice the lower-octave Bm scale below with free stroke *p-i* alternation. Use small, well-controlled *p* strokes alternating smoothly with the *i* strokes, like left and right windshield wipers. Because *p-i* alternation requires no change of hand position, it's usually the best way to play short melodic passages on the bass strings.

Fernando Sor has been called the "Beethoven of the guitar," and even his smaller pieces suggest why. This beautiful composition captures the serenity that Beethoven's slower, quieter pieces are famous for and reflects how the key of Bm itself helps to create that mood.

Lento

Fernando Sor
(1778–1839)

"Dropped D" Tuning

For music in the keys of D and Dm, the sixth string is often tuned down to low D. With the string tuned a whole step lower, its notes will be two frets *higher* than in standard tuning:

To tune down by ear, lower the string to well *below* D. Then, bring it back up *slowly* while playing it alternately with the open D string. As the sixth string tightens, listen for the clash of overtones to flatten out until you hear a single "thick" D tone with no dissonant oscillations.

Memorize and practice these lower-octave D major and minor scales using *p-i* alternation. For further thumb development and enhanced musicianship, accent the first beat of each measure by using rest strokes. Cultivating rest strokes with *p* provides various benefits in musical control.

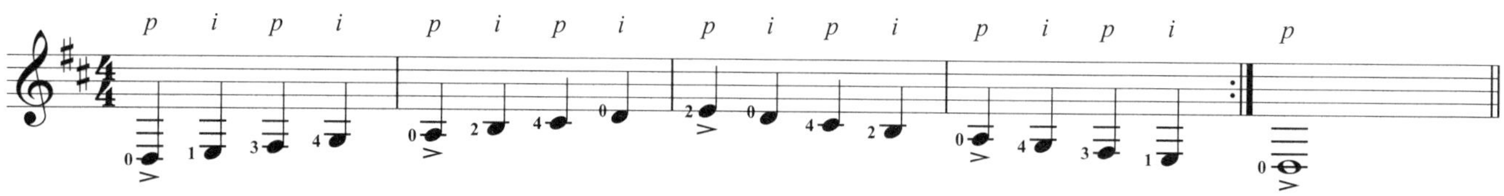

The dropped-D, two-octave major scale provides a good opportunity for learning how to play *m-i* bass-string notes without the ugly sound of nail-scraping. First, memorize it; then, practice with the technique explained below for changing the angle of your strokes.

CHANGING YOUR ANGLE OF ATTACK IN SCALE PLAYING

The illustrations here show the range of angles to the strings your *m-i* strokes can make, from perpendicular to around 30 degrees from perpendicular. Changes of angle are produced by *tiny* changes of wrist-curvature, and by varying your attack as shown, you can equalize the tone on the treble strings: angled to the full extent for string 1, slightly less for string 2, and still less for string 3. By continuing this process on the bass strings, you can *also* eliminate the scratchy tone produced by the friction between your nails and the metal string-winding. When you get to the fifth and sixth strings, the perpendicular stroke will be *parallel* with the metal winding, so that even these strings won't scrape against your nails. (You'll save wear and tear on your nails, too.)

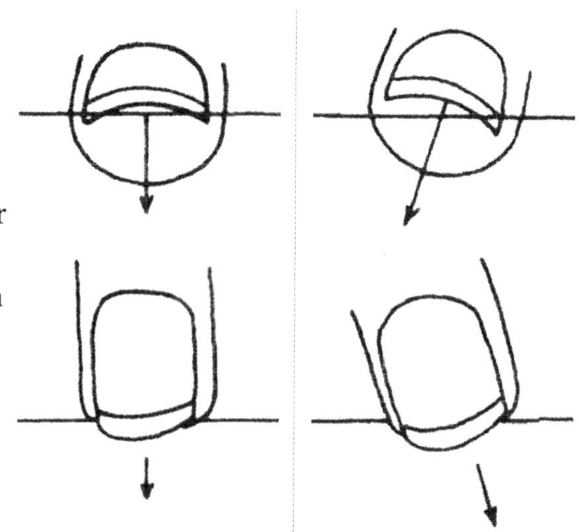

6th string attack *1st string attack*

Many fine Renaissance lute pieces are by unknown composers, and this is one of the best. The *gigue* (known in England as the "jig") was a very fast dance, normally in triple meter, that in the Baroque era became the standard concluding piece for instrumental suites (see p. 50). In order to play it confidently, master it first at half speed, with graceful, economical left-hand movements, solid right-hand stroke-preparations, and perfect synchronization of the hands on chord changes.

Kemp's Jig

Anonymous
(16th-century England)

USING HINGE BARRES

The tip-joint hinge barre you used on page 24 illustrated the value of hinge barres to sustain a bass note while playing an open first- or second-string melody note. When these needs are reversed, you can use the underside of your *knuckle* joint, as shown, to play the treble note while playing the open bass string. Then, clamp down the *lower* part of your finger for the subsequent bass note. In the next piece, both types are used in measure 9; instructions for playing them are at the bottom of the page.

The composer of "Bianco Fiore" (Italian, "white flower") was a 16th-century Italian dance-master whose compositions were transmitted to the modern world by the musicologist Oscar Chilesotti and made famous among guitarists by Andrés Segovia's recordings. The short trills called for in measures 4 and 12 are written out in footnotes 1 and 2 beneath the music.

✔ **TIP:** This version is somewhat closer to the original lute music than the Segovia and Parkening recordings.

Bianco Fiore

Cesare Negri
(c.1535–1605)

*On the first beat, use the underside of your knuckle-joint as shown in the photograph to play the 1st-string F♯ while simultaneously playing the open D. On the second beat, clamp down the rest of your finger to make the Bm chord. Then, on beat 3, hinge up on your fingertip to play the open E while sustaining the bass B through the bar line.

The "Sarabande" from Weiss's beautiful *Sonata 34* calls for a relaxed, flexible tempo to express its intense emotion. The slowest dance form of the times, the *sarabande* typically served as the slow movement in Baroque instrumental suites. The trills called for in the music are written out below the piece and numerically keyed to the places where they're used. (Note that the *first* is used only on the *repeat* of the A section.)

Sarabande

S.L. Weiss
(1686–1750)

⑥ = D

Adagio M.M. ♩ = 66

Damping (Muting) Techniques

As in the "Estudio" by Dionisio Aguado (p. 11), damping is used to honor the musical silences which sometimes are part of a composition. Its other most typical use is to eliminate overlapped bass-string sonorities when they create harmonic confusion or spoil a melodic line in the bass.

[1] The most intuitive, efficient way to silence unwanted resonance from the *next lower* bass string is the one introduced on page 8. That is, you use the *left side* of the thumb-tip by sandwiching it between the strings for just an instant as it makes nail contact with the higher string.

[2] The other way is to reach back and touch the vibrating string lightly with the tip of the thumb right *after* playing the new note. It's also the best way when the string to be damped isn't the *next* lower one—for example, the E string after playing the D string.

✔ **TIP:** Look at the illustration on page 6 of how *p* recovers from a free stroke. The *damping movement* is essentially the same as this natural *recovery movement.*

The examples below illustrate both methods. The second method permits the previous note to overlap the new note slightly, but by such a small fraction that it's not even noticeable.

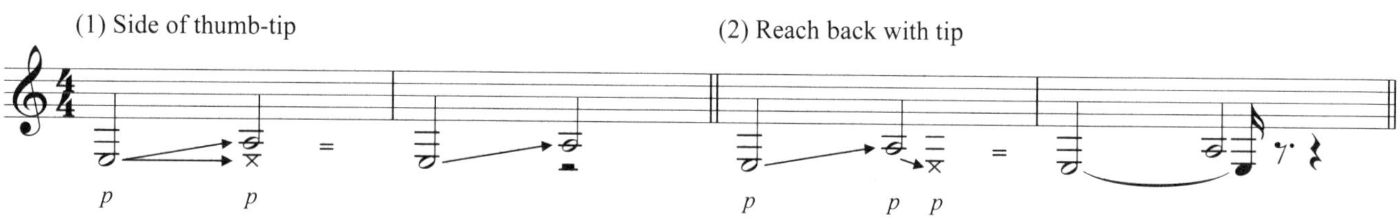

[3] To damp the next *higher* bass string, **(a)** you can use a rest stroke with *p* when the thumb is playing by itself, as in arpeggios. If it's playing together with other fingers, as in a chord, **(b)** you can "bounce" the thumb-tip up onto the higher string as a modification of its recovery. **(c)** The back of a *left*-hand fingertip also can be used when the next note to be fingered is on the *next lower* string. For a chord, **(d)** you can even add the finger that *would* play that string in the standard whole-chord formation but isn't needed in the music. The examples below illustrate each of these techniques except for **(c)**, which is explained further on the next page.

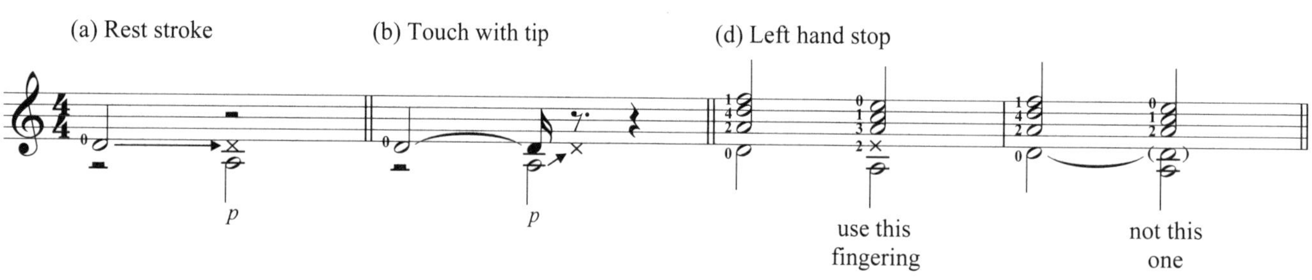

[4] Occasionally, an open *treble* string will need damping. In such cases, either **(a)** pre-planting with *a* or *a-m*, or **(b)** using the back of a *left*-hand fingertip works well, depending on the situation. These techniques are so intuitive that many players use them unconsciously to keep their melodic lines clean; both are discussed further on the next page, where we'll revisit Purcell's "Minuet" (p. 16) as a practice model. There are *ten* numbered places where a note will over-ring the next unless damped; solutions are listed numerically below the music.

Henry Purcell
(1659–1695)

[1] To keep the open E from over-ringing the D, plant *a* together with *m* on strings 1 and 2, which also prepares *a* for the *next* E (method [4a] from previous page).

[2] To keep the open D from blurring the C, "kiss" the fourth string with the back of your third finger as it "plants" to hold down the C (method [3c]).

[3] To prevent a harmonic clash with the implied B♭ chord here, kiss the open E with the back of your fourth fingertip as it makes the second-string D (method [4b]).

[4] As you plant *p-i-a* for the F chord, use the left side of your thumb-tip to silence the fifth-string A from the preceding measure (method [1]).

[5] Once again, the strong resonance of the open E needs to be stopped to prevent dissonance—here, with the implied Dm chord. The best way is to plant *a* along with *p* and *i*, leaving it planted for the E in the *next* measure while you play the notes in between (variation on method [4a]).

[6] Here, damping is *not needed* since note decay will minimize the lower string overlap. Also, the faint sonority of the A will reinforce nicely the implied Dm chord which ends the section.

[7] To play this important rest, plant *p* for the D on the *next* beat as *a* plants for the first-string A.

[8] Here, kiss the D string with the back of your first fingertip as it makes the C♯ bass—an easy left-hand bass-stop using method [3c].

[9] Likewise, silence the D with the back of your *third* fingertip as it frets the fifth-string C (method [3c]).

[10] Here, damping the A *is* necessary in order to provide a clean entry for the D.C. al Fine. Just lean your thumb back when planting *p* and *m* so that it momentarily touches the A string (method [1]).

If all of this sounds like a tall order, just take each occasion for damping by itself without worrying about the rest! The effort is primarily mental, and where the mind leads, the fingers will follow. By gradually applying these techniques to other pieces, you'll polish your performance style and take your command of dynamic preparations and goal-directed movements to a yet higher level.

The Keys of A Major and F# Minor

The key signatures of A major and F# minor use three sharps—F#, C#, and G#. Because of its pleasing middle register and the readily available open strings, A major is often used in classical guitar music. Memorize and practice the following second- and fifth-position scales and cadences.

TIP: The second-position scale form is the same as the fifth-position C scale (p. 20), but the fingering differs slightly to make up for the wider fret spaces. Instead of using a fourth finger extension to play the lower octave G#, it's easier and more effective to use pivot shifts to first position and back.

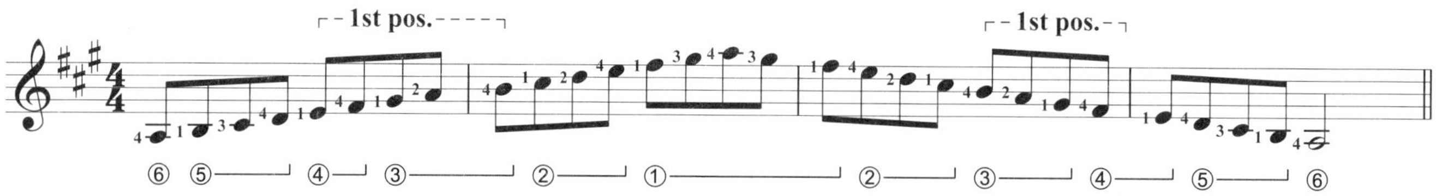

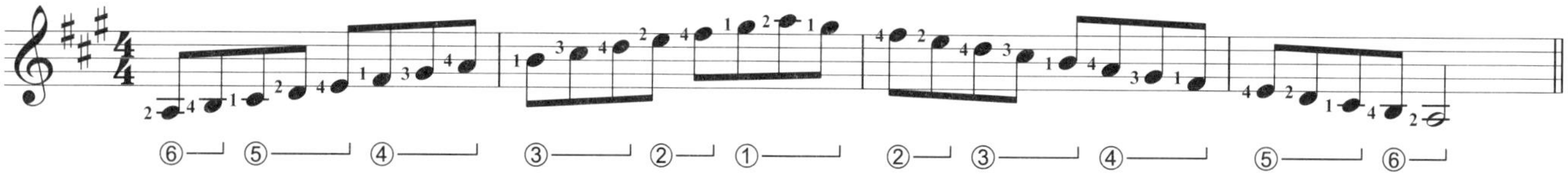

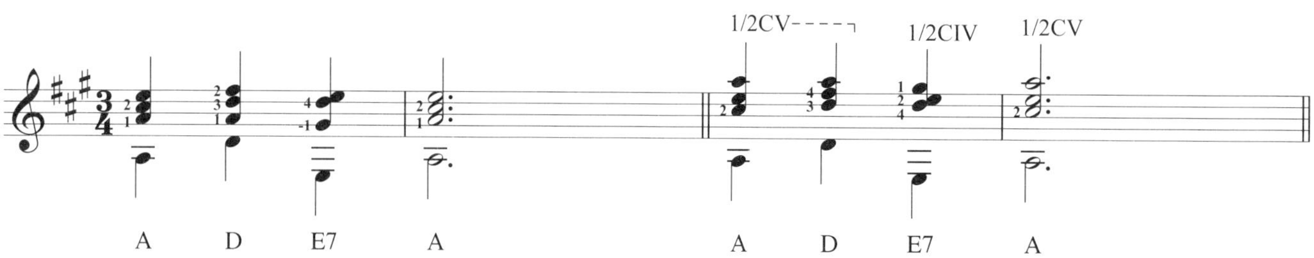

F# minor is not a home key for classical guitar music, but incidental use of it occurs from time to time, as in the “Gigue” on page 50. To gain familiarity with this key, memorize and practice the following F#m scales: **(1)** the first-position scale, which uses a conventional fingering with open strings; and **(2)** the second-position movable scale, used for other minor keys as well (for example, the seventh-position Bm scale on p. 52).

(1) First-position scale

(2) Second-position movable scale

Memorize and practice the previous cadences in the following arpeggiated forms:

John Dowland was the greatest of the lutenist-composers who flourished during the English Renaissance—the "golden age" of English music, as it's called. Much of his best music is melancholy-sounding; this piece is a fine example of his more playful moods. The rhythm contains a variety of figurations, so be sure to count accurately when you're learning it.

Mistress Winter's Jump

John Dowland
(1563–1626)

A contemporary of Bach and Weiss, Giuseppe Antonio Brescianello was an Italian Baroque composer whose works included a collection of 18 partitas for *colascione*, an Italian lute tuned like the guitar. The "Gigue" below is a good example of the many fine pieces in the collection and provides a great workout for both hands. Observe the fingering carefully, including how the A string in measures 4 and 16 is damped—the method described in [**3d**], page 46.

Gigue

G.A. Brescianello
(1690–1758)

The following composition is based on the romantic French bistro music of the earlier 20th century—the musical culture that produced such legendary artists as Edith Piaf and Django Reinhardt. The most popular all-purpose bistro instrument was the charming small accordion known as a *concertina*, and the piece is designed to capture its characteristic performance style.

Bistro Waltz

Charles Duncan

The Seventh Position

As the fifth position is the anchor position of the upper fingerboard, the seventh is the pivotal position. Besides serving as a secure way-station between the fifth and ninth positions, it's used commonly for guitar music in several keys. The new notes are at the 9th and 10th frets as shown:

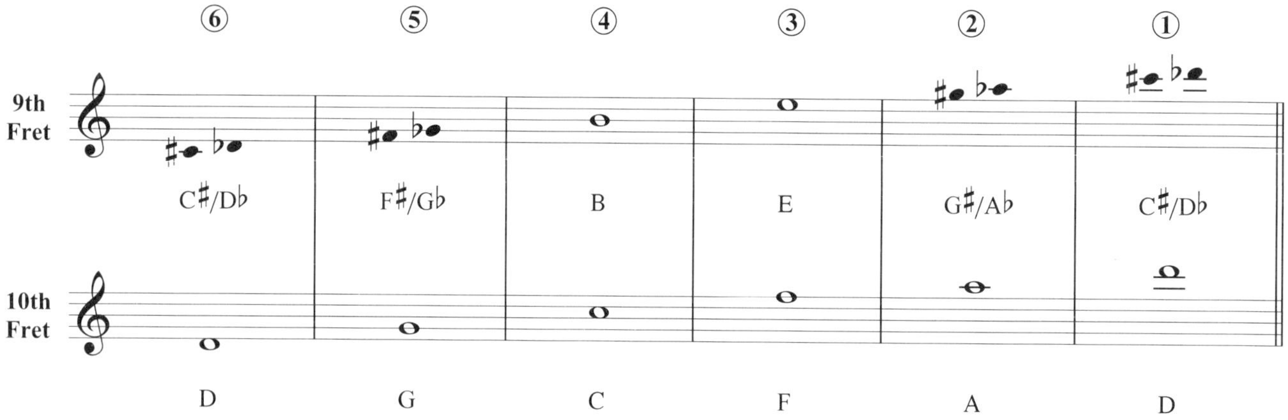

To get well-acquainted with the seventh position, practice the following two-octave D, Bm, and C scales using conscious GDM. (Their scale *forms* are the same ones you learned on page 48.)

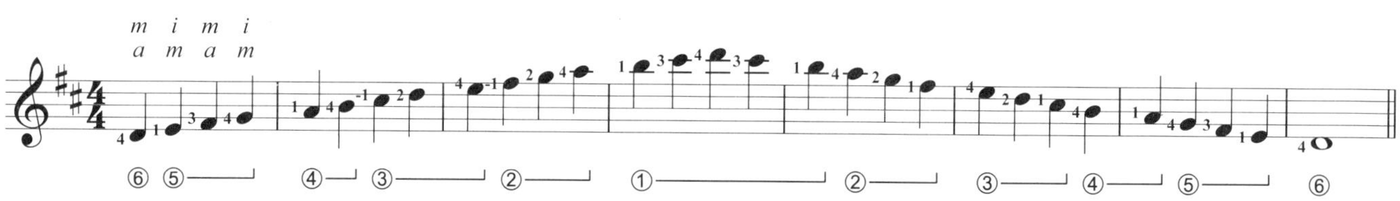

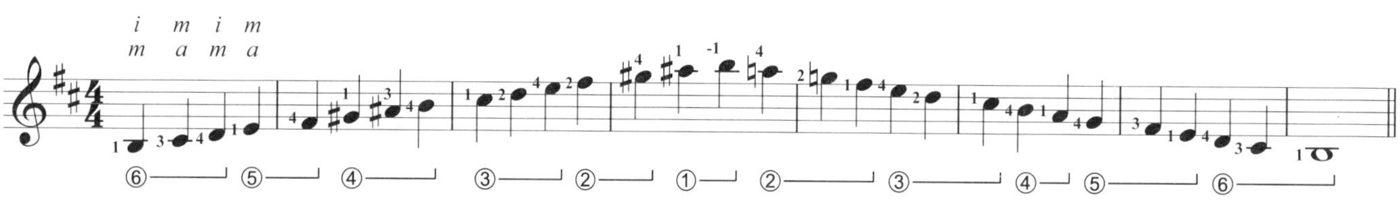

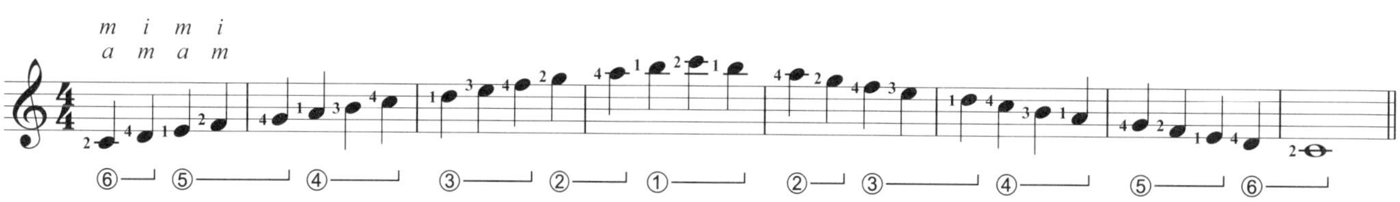

Practicing Beethoven's famous "Ode to Joy" (Book One, p. 33) in the interesting split-octave melodic format below will also help accustom you to seventh position as a secure home base.

In this small masterpiece by Sor, you'll be using seventh position and also a **slide-slur** with your fourth finger on beat 4 of measure 9 (see the asterisk). This easy technique is used all the time by steel-string players and has uses in classical guitar playing as well.

TIP: To make the two-fret slide from G to A sound as clean as the hammer-on that precedes it, use yet another form of GDM. Aim your slide for the *6th* metal fret as a *backstop*, and increase the *pressure* on your fingertip as it crosses the *5th* fret.

Andantino

Fernando Sor
(1778–1839)

M.M. ♩ = 120

This great Mexican folk classic provides a good fifth- and seventh-position workout because of how the melody is harmonized—*thirds* in the "A" section and *sixths* in the "B" section. It also introduces you to the kinds of Spanish harmony and rhythm you'll be playing later (pp. 72–75).

La Llorona

Traditional Mexican
arr. Charles Duncan

OTHER USES OF THE HIGHER POSITIONS: NATURAL HARMONICS

Harmonics are chime-like tones produced by lightly touching a string right above the metal fret. **Natural harmonics** are available at the 4th, 5th, 7th, 9th, 12th, and 18th frets. By using the more advanced technique of **artificial harmonics**, they can be played also at the other frets (see p. 76).

Harmonics are written in the form of diamond-shaped notes an octave *lower* than their actual pitch and identified by the abbreviation "Arm." (Spanish, *armonico*) plus their fret number in Roman numerals. The notes you can produce effectively with this technique are shown below:

Arm. XII

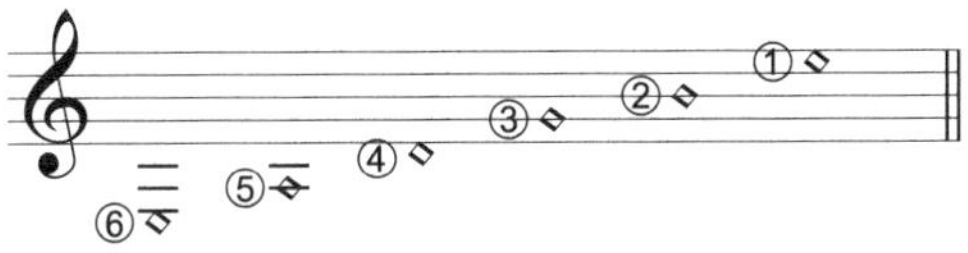

Arm. VII & XVIII

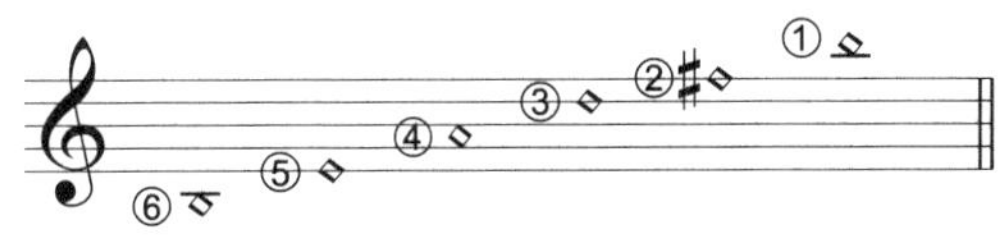

Arm. V

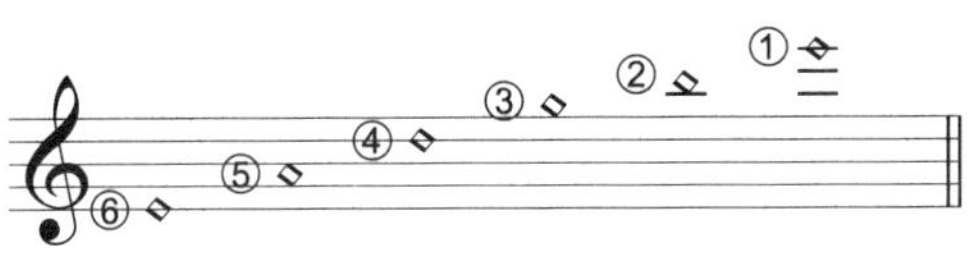

Arm. IV & IX

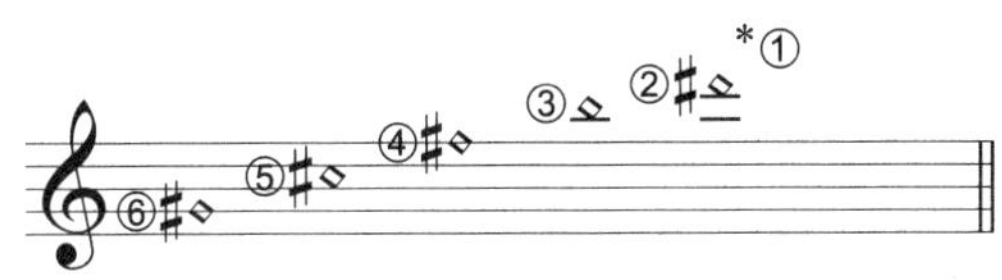

*No usable harmonics on string 1.

Harmonics at the 12th fret are the easiest to execute cleanly. Follow the steps below to learn how, starting with the D string—it's the most responsive for this purpose.

[1] *Touch* the string with the fleshy underside of your second finger's tip-joint, *not* the tip itself.

[2] Make sure the fingertip is directly *over* the metal fret, not behind it as in normal playing.

[3] Pluck the string close to the bridge and *immediately* afterwards lift the fingertip off the string.

[4] Practice on the other strings until you can produce clear, consistent "chimes"; then do the same for harmonics at the other frets. For the clearest sound, always pluck close to the bridge.

Tuning with Natural Harmonics

As shown below, bass-string harmonic notes at the *5th* fret reappear at the *7th* fret on the next higher string. Notice also that the *7th*-fret B and E on strings 6 and 5 are exactly the same pitches as the open second and first strings. These natural matching-tones provide an excellent way to tune your guitar accurately, assuming your *6th* string is tuned to the correct pitch.

Arm. V = Arm. VII

[1] 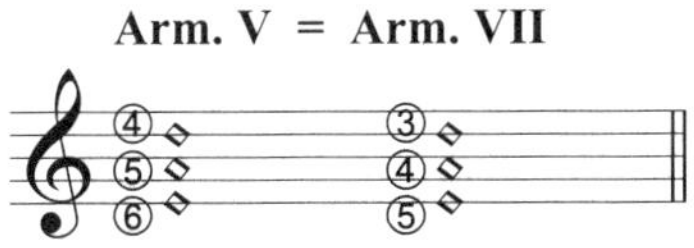

Arm. VII = open strings

[2] 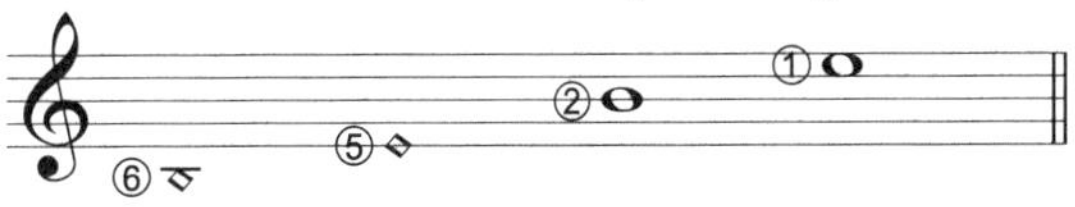

[1] To tune strings 5, 4, and 3, pluck the 5th-fret harmonic on the next *lower* string, and while it's still ringing, pluck the *7th*-fret harmonic on the string to be tuned. With both harmonics still ringing, adjust the higher string's tuning key while listening for a perfect match with no dissonant oscillations. Repeat until you hear only a single "thick" tone.

[2] To tune the second and first strings, use the same procedure to match their natural pitches with the corresponding 7th-fret harmonics—string 6 for the B string and string 5 for the E string.

The Keys of E Major and C♯ Minor

The keys of E major and C♯ minor have four sharps as their key signatures—F♯, C♯, G♯, and D♯. Despite the number of sharps, E major is one of the best classical guitar keys because of the many open-string fingerings you can use and the extra resonance they afford. Memorize and practice the following two-octave first-position scale and fourth-position extended one-octave scale.

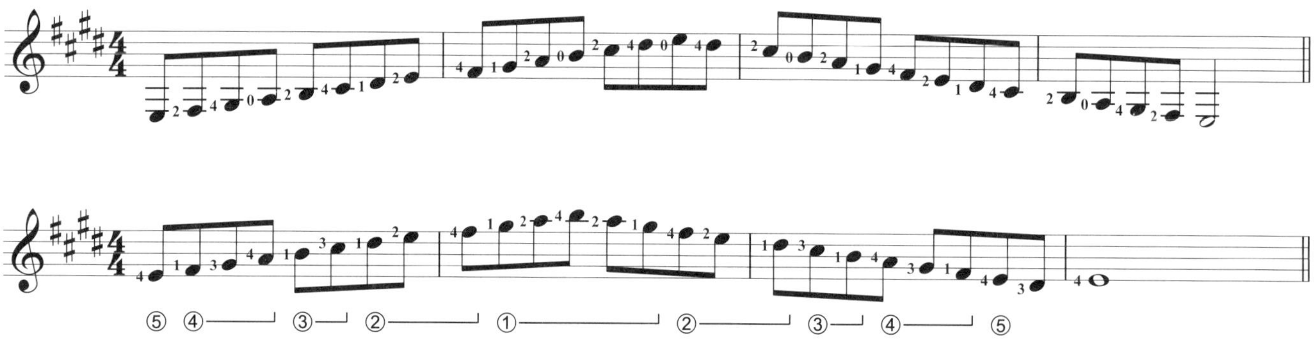

Memorize and practice their corresponding cadences with GDM. Practice the first one *also* as the *p-i-m-a-m-i* exercise shown, concentrating on your "sticky-fingered" planting technique which makes the fingers feel like they're chained together (see again pp. 9, 32).

Like F♯m, C♯m is not a home key in classical guitar music, but incidental use of it is common—for example, in measures 10–12 of the duet on page 58. Memorize and practice the following two-octave C♯m scale—it's also a movable scale form used in other keys as well.

Carcassi's lively "Waltz" makes an enjoyable introduction to music in the key of E, and although not difficult, measures 9–12 are tricky—they'll need extra practice. In the long "B" section, use the half-rest stroke to make the melody *sing* (see again pp. 24, 28). On the dramatic leaps from F♯ to B (at the asterisks), **[1]** dynamically prepare the shift with your elbow's backswing on the F♯, **[2]** lead off with it on the open B, **[3]** fix your gaze on the fourth *position* (not just the 7th *fret!*) as the target, with your first finger as an anchor on G♯, and **[4]** finish with a *full* rest stroke on the climax tone (the high B).

Waltz

Matteo Carcassi
(1792–1853)

Like the stylistically similar "Ode to Joy" in Beethoven's Ninth Symphony, the triumphant theme of the finale to Brahms's First Symphony is one of the greatest song-tunes in orchestral music. On the repeat, play it somewhat louder and a tiny bit faster to dramatize the feeling of sublime, heroic courage which Brahms conveys so well in musical language.

Theme from the First Symphony

Johannes Brahms
(1833–1897)

"Cavaquinho" ("kahva-*keen*-yo"—a small Brazilian folk guitar) is based on the universally popular Brazilian jazz style known as *bossa nova*. Since it's quite syncopated, count the rhythm aloud while playing until you're comfortable with it. (For further practice in playing syncopated modern music, see the author's *Pop Classics for Fingerstyle Guitar* [Hal Leonard].)

Cavaquinho

Allegretto M.M. ♩ = 88

Charles Duncan

Attitudes of the Left Hand: Longitudinal and Lateral Configurations

Let's recall the two principles of a dynamically prepared left-hand position as introduced on page 5: **(1)** The natural alignment of the hand and forearm which provides maximum strength and comfort. **(2)** The longitudinal spread of well-curved fingers which balances the hand, channels leverage to the weaker third and fourth fingers, and provides easy coverage of a whole fingerboard position.

Now it's time to add a third—the way you move easily and naturally from *longitudinal* attitudes of the fingers, such as the Gmaj7 pictured below, to more *lateral* configurations like the D9 chord to its right. How can that be done *without* a stressful bending and curving of the wrist?

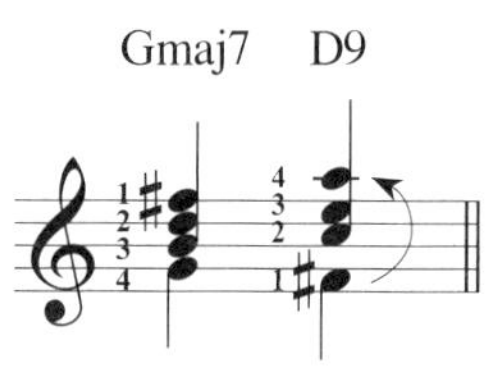

(1) Rotate out, ab*duct elbow*

(2) Rotate in, ad*duct elbow*

The secret is to keep a *loose arm.* Rather than abandon the natural alignment of the hand and forearm, combine forearm rotation with some elbow play. **(1)** For the change from Gmaj7 to D9, use a quarter-turn of *outward* rotation, accompanied by a slight abduction of the elbow away from the body. **(2)** For the return to Gmaj7, use the equivalent *inward* rotation, supported by a slight *ad*duction of the elbow back toward the body. In the photographs and musical illustrations above, the arrows indicate how efficiently the hand and fingers are torqued into the correct position by this leverage from a loose arm. Use the following exercise to practice the movements correctly.

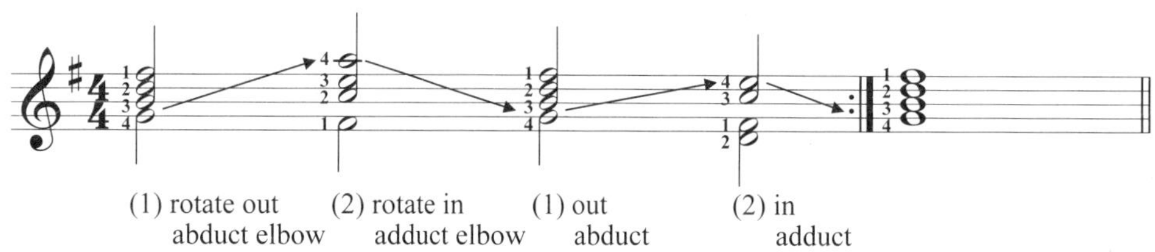

These techniques apply to any situation in which you need to change back and forth between comparable configurations. The next exercise, which uses the fingers in pairs (1 and 3, 2 and 4), is a good example. Practice until you can play it smoothly with the supportive movements indicated.

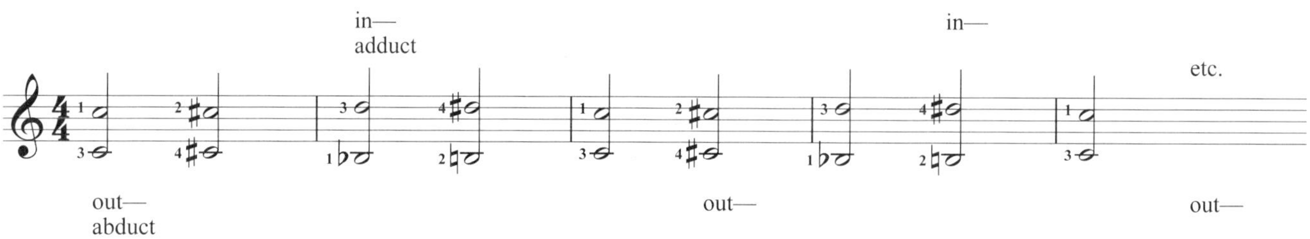

TIP: Hold down each pair of fingers until the next pair completes its exchange movement and is touching the strings. At no time should *both* pairs of fingers lose contact with the fingerboard!

INCREASING LEFT-HAND STRENGTH AND AGILITY

Besides slur and scale pattern exercises, there are exercises designed specifically to develop left-hand strength and agility. On this page and the next, you'll learn some of the most valuable.

The "Spider"

This exercise is named for the way the fretting hand looks like a tarantula crawling up the fingerboard. In each cycle, the paired fingers exchange configurations just as in the previous exercise, assisted by the same "loose arm" technique. Practice in first position as shown in the first line of music. For variety and endurance, ascend chromatically to seventh position as shown in the *second* line.

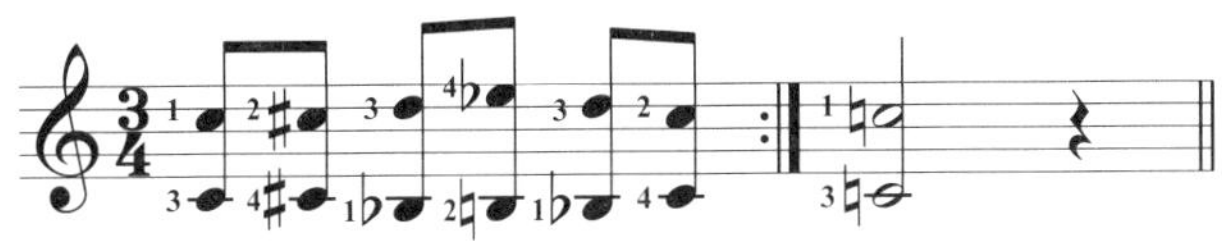

Chromatic Octave Scales

You'll gain additional strength and agility by practicing exercises based on the first-position chromatic octave scale. First, memorize and practice the scale with careful GDM, being sure to hold down the notes just played until the next pair of fingers touches the strings. As in the "Spider," use the correct forearm and elbow movements to support your hand and finger action.

When the scale is memorized, practice the following pattern exercise. When it's memorized as well, try constructing a few more for yourself. Inventing pattern exercises will strengthen your mental command of left-hand movements and your ability to think ahead.

BARRED CHORD PRACTICE

As noted earlier (p. 13), building up the muscles between your thumb and forefinger will improve your barred chord expertise dramatically. The following exercise is great for that purpose, and also provides excellent arpeggio practice. When you can play it cleanly, add the four patterns following it to your practice and then try inventing some of your own for more variety. Within a few weeks, you'll see real gains in strength, plus a more dynamic arpeggio technique.

Alternative Arpeggio Patterns

Ninth Position and Beyond

The terminal position of the free fingerboard is the ninth, and besides the 9th- and 10th-fret notes you learned in seventh position, it includes the following layout of 11th- and 12th-fret notes. Notice that the 12th-fret notes are the same as the open strings but an octave higher:

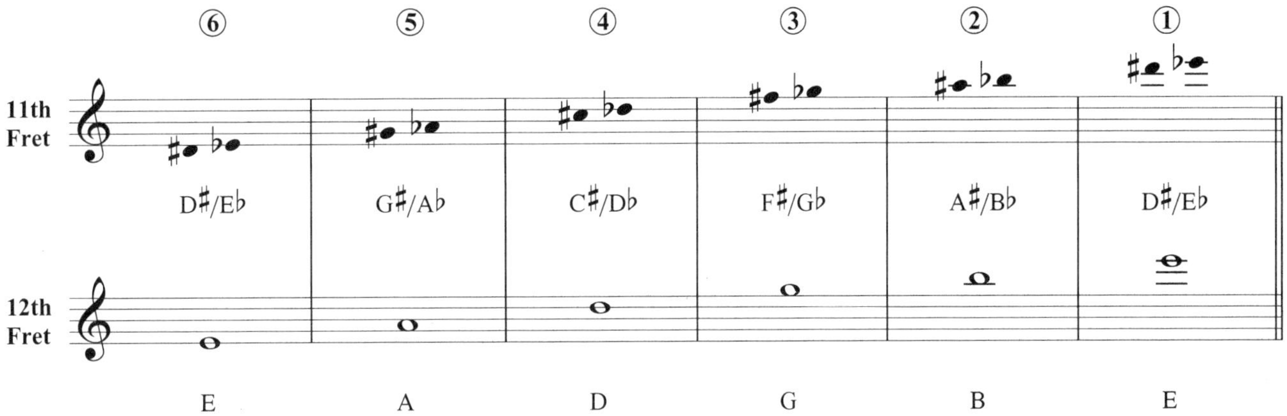

The following notes beyond the 12th fret are available on the first string and require a relocation of the hand to where the neck of the guitar joins the body. Although most of the guitar repertoire doesn't go beyond ninth or tenth position, you'll occasionally see these highest notes in advanced level compositions.

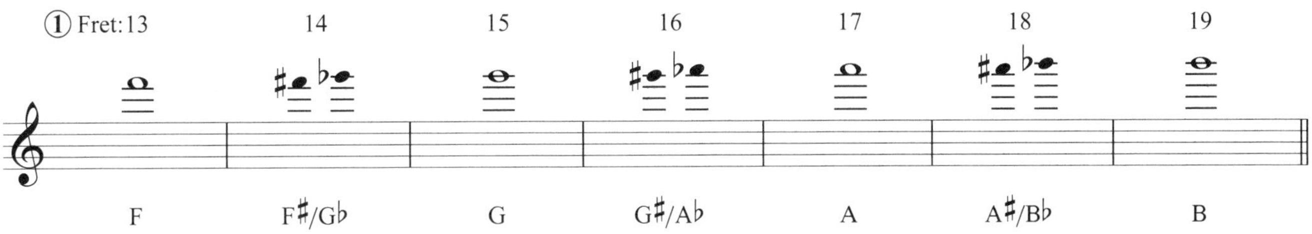

Memorize and practice the following ninth-position scales: **(1)** the two-octave D major scale and **(2)** the extended one-octave A major scale. **(3)** Then do the same for the two-octave E major scale, which begins in *sixth* position and shifts to ninth position for the higher octave.

(1)

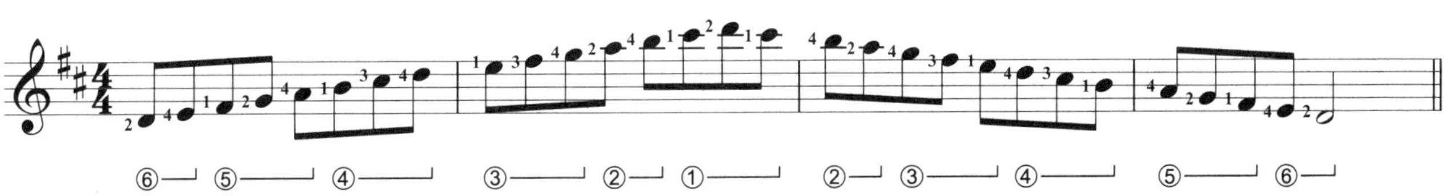

(2)

(3)

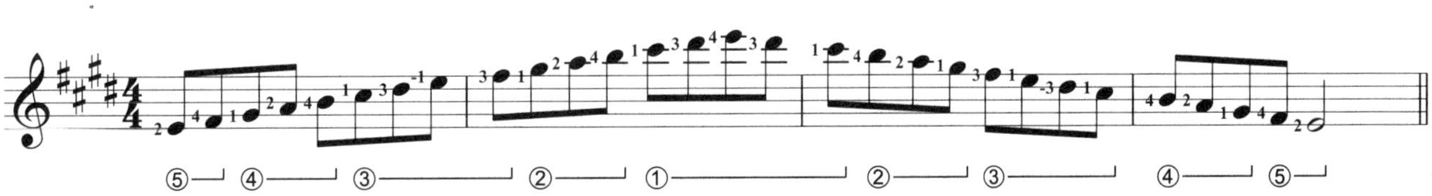

What better way to get used to playing in ninth position than with the most famous classical guitar solo of all time? First recorded in 1897, during the 20th century it gained international popularity as a concert classic and motion picture theme. It's also known in several different versions, but the one below is the most traditional, including the title (Spanish for "Anonymous Romance").

[1] Practice it *first* in the form of block chords as shown below. In the process, you'll see that the E *major* "B" section will need extra work—especially the shifts. Also, in its fourth measure, notice the C double sharp—it's the same tone as a D natural. However, for correct musical spelling, **double sharps** (𝄪) and **double flats** (𝄫) are used in the sharp and flat keys, respectively.

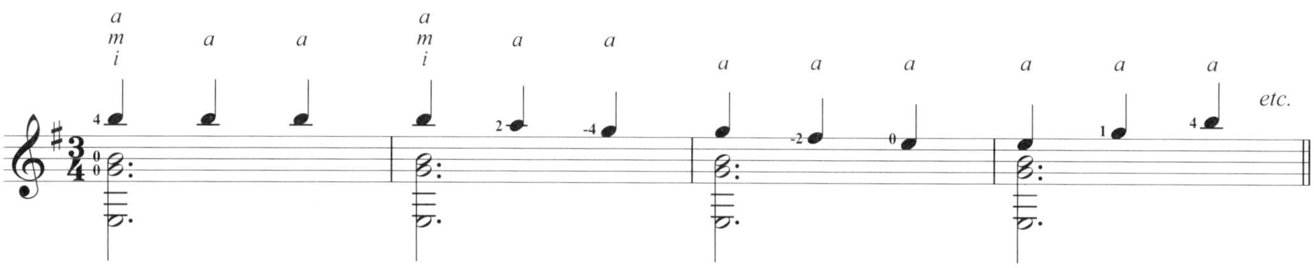

[2] Next, work on it with *precise* sequential planting so that each finger in the cycle feels like it's being pulled quickly into its prepared position by a strong magnetic attraction. Be sure also that *p* and *a* plant simultaneously just before the first beat of each measure, and in the case of position shifts, before the left hand leaves the chord it's holding.

[3] Finally, accent the melody as indicated in the first measure. Although this is customarily done with rest strokes on each melody note throughout the piece, an equally valid approach is to use mainly *half*-rest strokes and save the full rest strokes for points of greater musical emphasis.

Romance Anonimo

Anonymous
Spanish

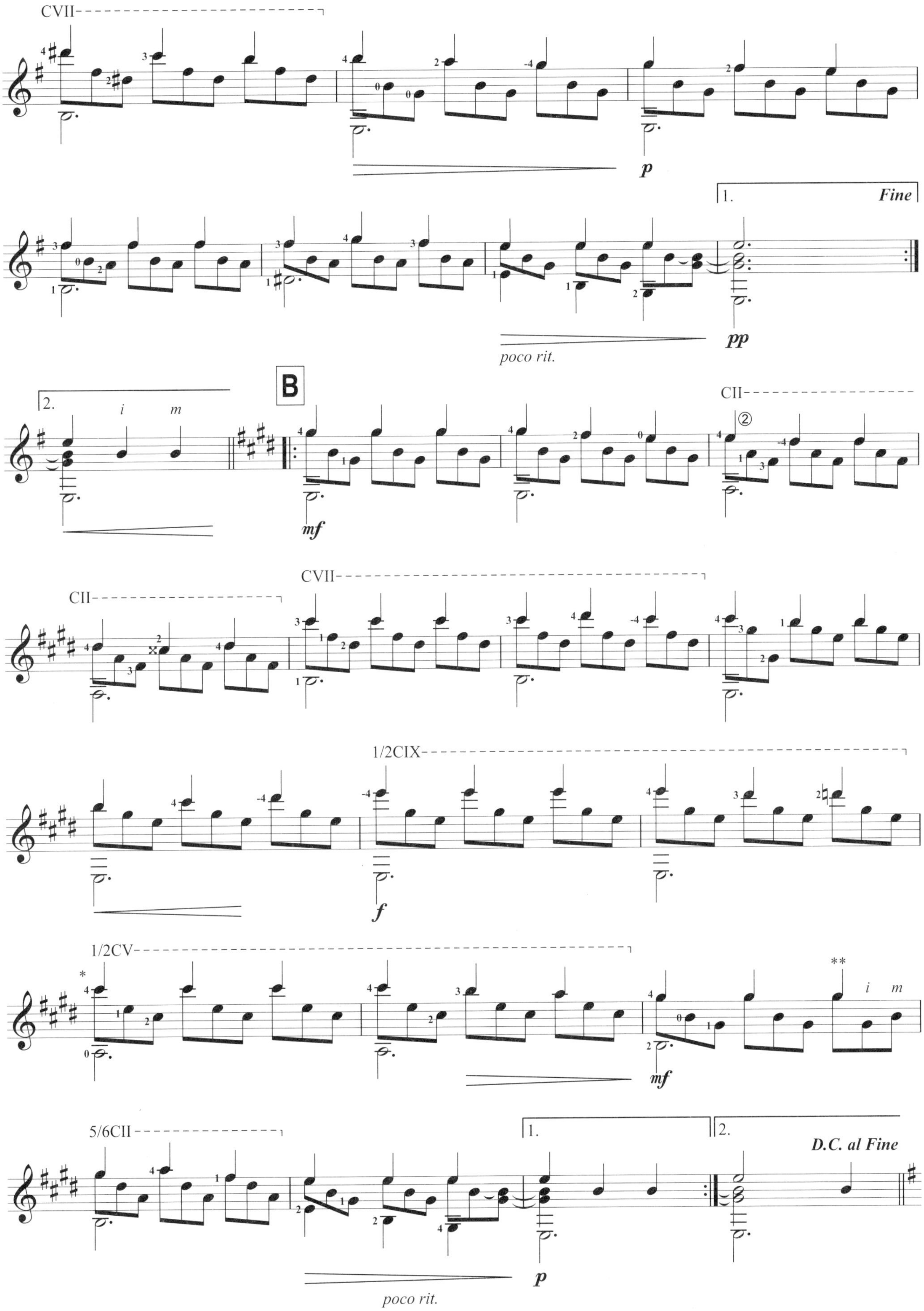

*This notoriously tricky shift can be cleaned up by separating the bass and treble as shown here, so that the open A neatly covers the shift. Be sure to play the A slightly *before* the beat and the C♯ *on* the beat to keep the rhythm intact.

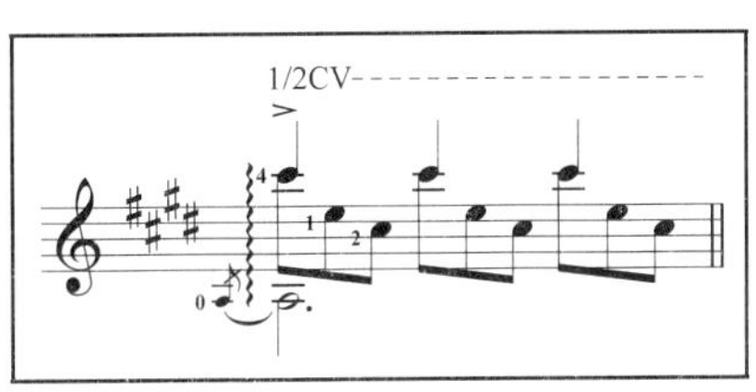

**This unobtrusive but effective reversal of the G♯ and B enables a much cleaner shift to the cadential B7 chord by covering the movement with the open B string.

Until they reach an advanced level, classical guitar students would probably think of Mauro Giuliani as the composer of numerous etudes and beginner-to-intermediate pieces. However, in his tragically short life, Giuliani also composed a huge body of concert music which has been rediscovered and recorded by many of the top players. The following short masterwork provides a gateway to that repertoire, as well as practice in using the highest positions of the fingerboard.

Andantino Grazioso

Mauro Giuliani
(1781–1829)

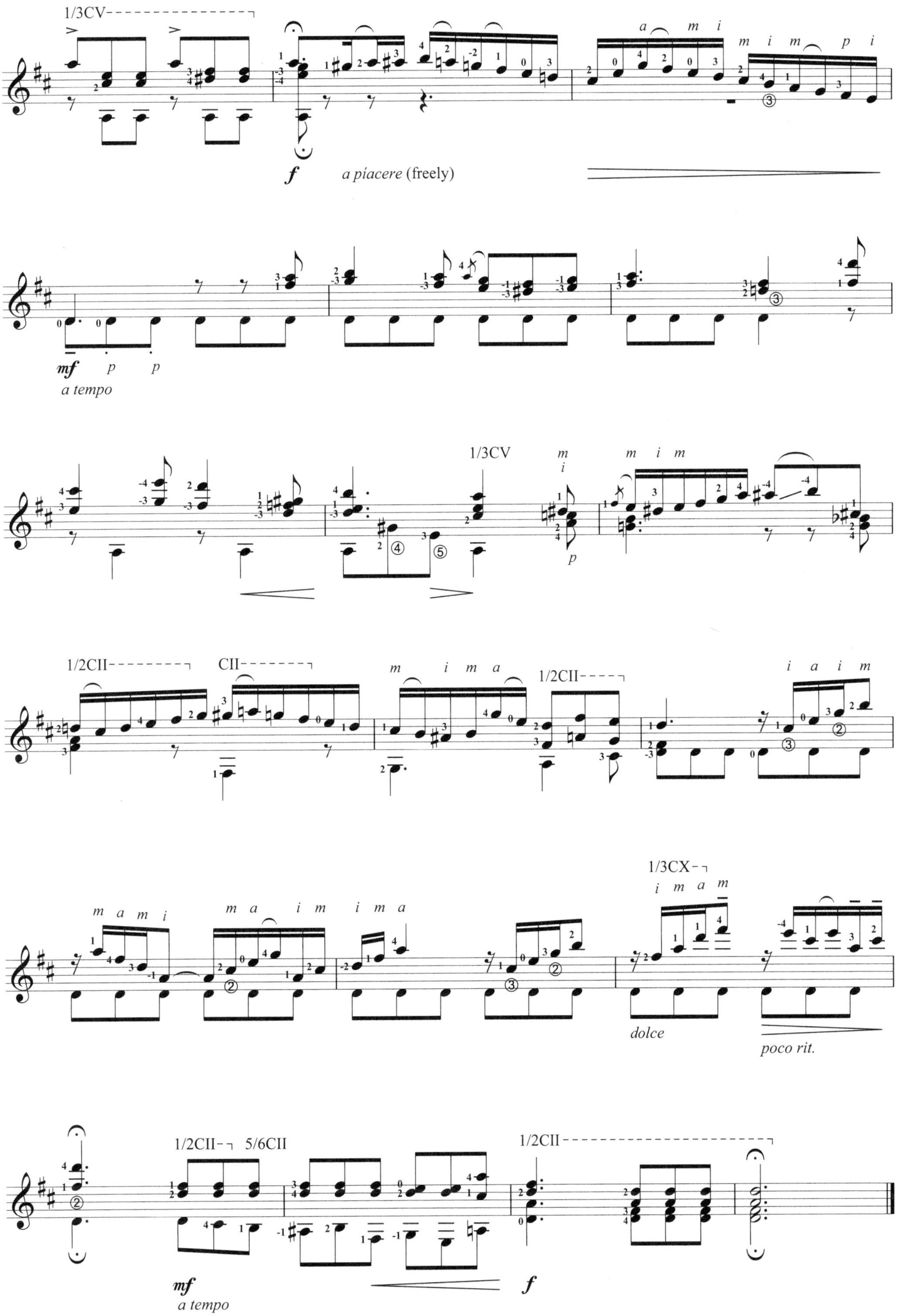
1/3CV
f
a piacere (freely)
mf
a tempo
1/3CV
1/2CII
CII
1/2CII
1/3CX
dolce
poco rit.
1/2CII
5/6CII
mf
a tempo
f
1/2CII

Although it doesn't make very much use of the upper fingerboard, the famous "Bourrée" from Bach's *Lute Suite No. 1* will challenge your technique and musicianship in various ways. Follow the practice scheme below as a guide to mastering this great piece.

BOURRÉE: STEPS TO MASTERY

[1] Practice with an enhanced GDM that includes two consecutive changes. Thus, as you play the first notes (E over G), visualize your left hand executing not just the F# bass and melody notes on the "and" of beat 4, but also the G over E across the bar line on beat *1*. Do likewise for the subsequent changes on beats 2 and 3 and keep going by counting and visualizing "four-and-*one*," "two-and-*three*." Break the piece into its well-defined four-measure phrases as practice units and look for some impressive gains in left-hand security and mental command after a few days.

[2] Fast contrapuntal pieces such as this will test your right-hand accuracy to the limit. Therefore, when practicing at 75% speed, plant more aggressively than usual in order to ensure right-hand security and precise right-hand/left-hand synchronization. Because of its residual imprint on motor memory, practicing with forceful, super-staccato articulations at 75% speed leads to more accurate, relaxed playing when this demand is lifted at performance speed.

[3] The articulation marks in the first two measures serve as a guide to phrasing the piece—"dit-dit-*dah*, dit-dit-*dah*," etc. However, when playing the downbeat quarter notes, play *no louder* than on the upbeat eighth notes—in fact, when practicing slowly, play them *softer* just to be sure. This will help you avoid the stiff, boring metric accents that are as instinctive as clapping, and contribute to the "long line" (i.e., the vocal quality) of the four-measure phrases.

[4] To offset the complex left-hand demands of this piece, you'll need to double down on your dynamically prepared chord-changing and shifting technique (pp. 8, 24, 60), especially in its more difficult passages. The *most* difficult is the dramatic four-measure conclusion, where the counterpoint is intensified by the close-packed overlapping motives in the bass and treble parts. This beautiful but risky grand finale will benefit the most from such practice in "super slo-mo."

[5] Embellishment is used for the three cadences where you'll see a short trill in small sixteenth notes tied to the principal tone. Play the trills and the concluding mordent (on the final E) as shown:

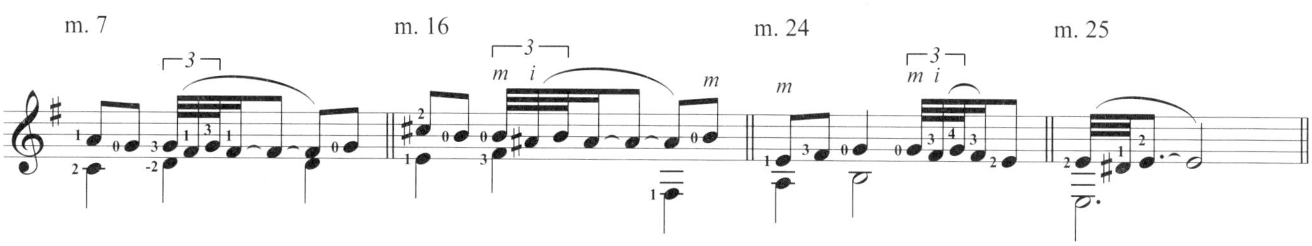

TIP: Note that the first trill is played entirely with a slur, while the second and third use the adjacent open string for the *first* note. This hybrid technique, used also in measure 8 of the Weiss "Sarabande" (p. 45), creates effective trills where neither pure slurring or cross-string trilling would be as easy or sound as good.

Bourrée

J.S. Bach
(1685–1750)

Allegro M.M. ♩ = 132

Right-Hand Development: Faster Scales and Arpeggios

In both hands, the secret of speed is the **economy of movement principle**—the less motion needed to accomplish a given task, the less time needed for it. Although you can increase left-hand economy by deliberately restraining excess movement, for the right hand, the easiest and most effective way is with staccato practice. When playing staccato, you automatically restrict the distance covered by the fingers by absorbing the recovery movement into your next preparation.

STACCATO PRACTICE WITH INCREASING METRONOME SETTINGS

[1] For both scales and arpeggio exercises, prepare each stroke decisively, with firm fingernail engagement. Increase the metronome settings until you can no longer distinguish between planting and playing, record your speed, and use it as a benchmark of your progress. Although maximum speed can't be increased voluntarily, *controlled* speed (i.e., with planting) definitely *can*, and for each gain in controlled speed, there's a small derivative gain in maximum speed.

[2] For practice models, use the following arpeggio pattern and one-octave G scale. Then, apply the technique to **(a)** various arpeggio exercises and pieces (pp. 9, 10, 25, 29, 32, 40, 48, 56, 62), and **(b)** scales and scale-pattern exercises (pp. 16, 19, 23, 32, 40, 48, 52, 56, 63).

Reflex-Based Modes of Dynamic Preparation

To complement your staccato practice, *reflex-based* forms of dynamic preparation are a great way to gain additional fluency. These include **(1)** dotted or staggered rhythms, and **(2)** speed bursts. Since they're reflex-based, you don't need to make any effort to plant—just take it for granted.

[1] The dotted and staggered rhythm exercises which follow can also be applied to the repertoire of scale and arpeggio exercises listed above. Practice them using these rhythmic formulas at progressively higher metronome settings.

✔ **TIP:** The ligatures you'll see in the music are *not* slurs or ties. They've been inserted to make the note-connections easier to see as tightly linked upbeat-downbeat groupings, irrespective of how they're beamed. Thus, in the first measure of exercises **(a)** and **(b)**, the way to count is "*One,*—ta-*Two,*—ta-*Three,*" etc.

(a)

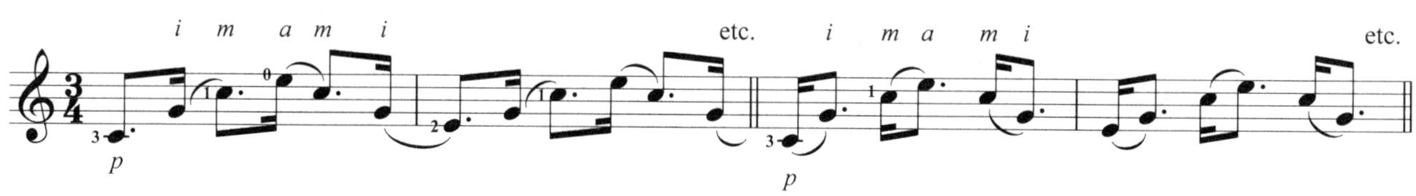

(b) 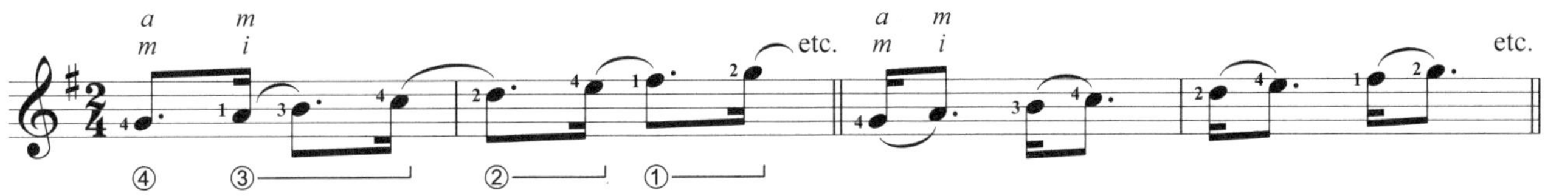

(c) 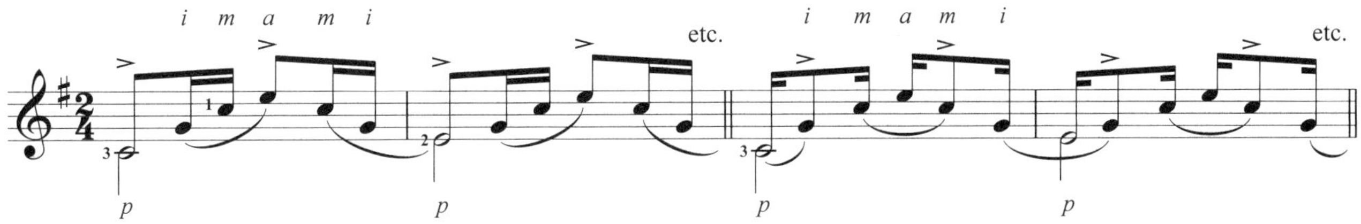

(d) 

[2] Speed bursts employ dynamic preparation in the form of micro-relaxations between groups of fast notes, comparable to the breaths taken between groups of arm-strokes in freestyle swimming. Practicing bursts like those below at increasing metronome settings will improve your overall fluency in playing scales and arpeggios, because you'll be learning to cluster several notes under a single playing impulse. With only one act of will needed to play all of them, there will be a net speed gain proportional to the savings in mental effort expended on their execution.

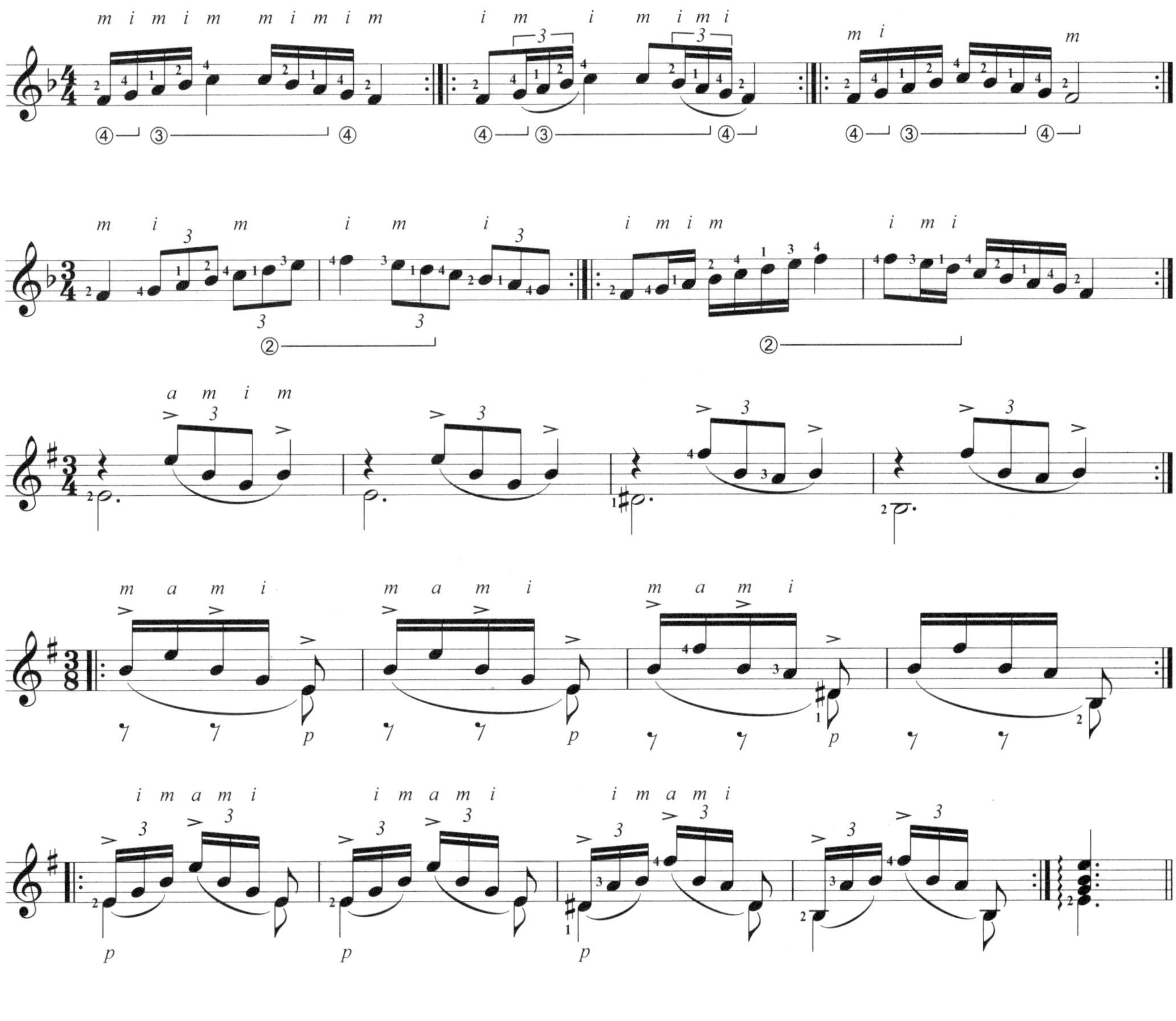

Flamenco Rasgueado

Book Two introduces students to flamenco playing—the Phrygian modes on which it's largely based, the basic *rasgueado* with *i*, and the *malaguena* as one of its most traditional dance forms. In this section, you'll be introduced to the next level of rasgueado playing, the use of hemiola as a rhythmic device, and another traditional dance form called the *peteneras.*

Like the up-and-down strokes with *i*, the basic four-finger flamenco "roll" is highly percussive and rhythmically exact. To play it, **(1)** anchor your thumb on the face of the guitar and clench your fingertips into the palm of your hand. **(2)** Starting with the little finger (*c*, for *chico*), *snap* the fingers out of your palm as shown below, making sure each finger comes to a full extension.

continue with *m*, then *i*

Note below that each finger strikes approximately three strings, and that the *c-a-m* strokes form a triplet which serves as an upbeat to the downbeat with *i*. Although often written this way, to save space, the broken chord symbol is also used. Thus, the second measure sounds just like the first.

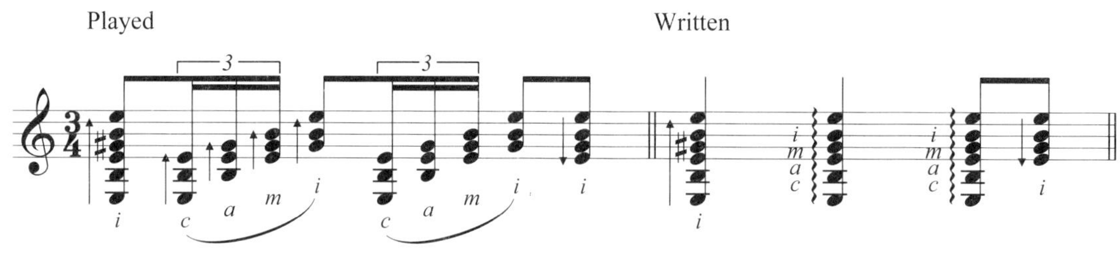

In addition to its use of the Phrygian mode and rasgueado technique, the rhythm of *peteneras* is based on hemiola, another typical feature of flamenco music. **Hemiola** consists of an alternation in triple meter between 3/4 and 6/8 rhythms, which only *looks* confusing. To play it correctly, simply count a steady beat in eighth notes (i.e., "1-2-3-4-5-6") with the note-groupings and accentuations shown below that make it alternately 6/8 (**1**-2-3, **4**-5-6) and 3/4 (**1**-2, **3**-4, **5**-6):

Count:	**1**	2	3 -	**4**	5	6	**1**	2 -	**3**	4 -	**5**	6
Sounds like:	**1** -	trip -	let,	**2** -	trip -	let	**1**	and,	**2**	and,	**3**	and

TIP: Practicing this rasgueado also serves as a valuable workout for the weak extensor muscles on the back of the hand. Although their only natural function is to open the hand, in classical guitar playing, they power the recovery from all finger-strokes. Rasgueado practice will strengthen them with a form of resistance-training that benefits your overall right-hand technique.

Peteneras

Traditional Flamenco

Like flamenco, the spirited folk classic "El Vito" comes from the Andalusian region of southern Spain, uses the Phrygian mode, and includes hemiola in its rhythm. Unlike "Peteneras," however, its notation is 3/4 throughout except in the middle and end of this arrangement, where it alternates with 2/4. This unusual meter *also* only looks confusing. Since quarter notes are exactly the same length in *both* time signatures, just use your metronome and play on each click. For how to count the hemiola, see the last line of music below.

TIP: In measure 7, you'll see a **cross-string slur**, another type which sometimes can be very useful. To play it, pluck the C on string 2 and hammer the B♭ on string 3 energetically and decisively. If your hammer-stroke is sufficiently percussive, the connection between the two notes will sound like a normal slur.

El Vito

Traditional Spanish
Arr. Charles Duncan

5/6CI
2/3CII
1/2CII
mf
poco rit.
a tempo
p
1.
2.
cresc. poco a poco
ff

Artificial Harmonics and Tremolo

You've learned how to play open-string harmonics by touching an open string over the frets where they naturally occur (p. 55). For *fretted notes*, you can create the node which divides a string into vibrating halves with your right hand alone. The resulting pitch is an octave above the fretted note, and notes played this way are known as **artificial harmonics**, or "octave harmonics." To learn the technique, follow these steps:

[1] With your left hand, finger the C♯ at the 2nd fret of the B string.

[2] As shown in the photograph, extend your *i* finger as if you were pointing and touch the string *twelve* frets higher at a point directly over the metal fret (here, the 14th fret of the B string).

[3] Simultaneously pluck the string with your *a* finger, as also indicated. Unlike normal free stroke, this specialized plucking action requires a curled finger and a flex from the middle joint.

[4] Immediately lift your *i* finger so that the harmonic can resonate freely.

[5] When you can play consistently clear harmonics, alternate between C♯ and the open-string B without watching your left hand. Keep your eyes on the tip of *i* as it switches back and forth between the 12th and 14th frets.

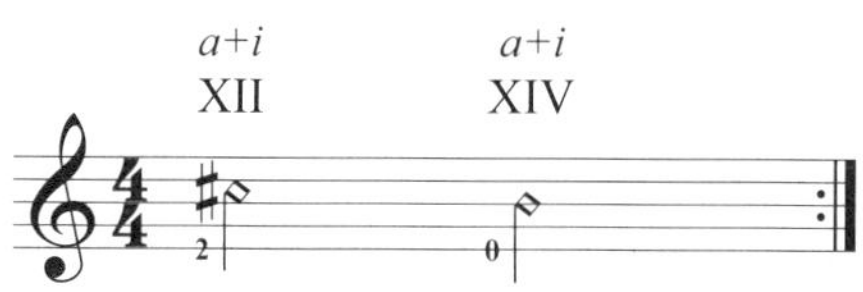

TIP: To produce a clear harmonic, make sure your *i* finger stays straight in order to maintain the proper distance between the *a* and *i* fingers, and also ensure solid tip-contact with *i*.

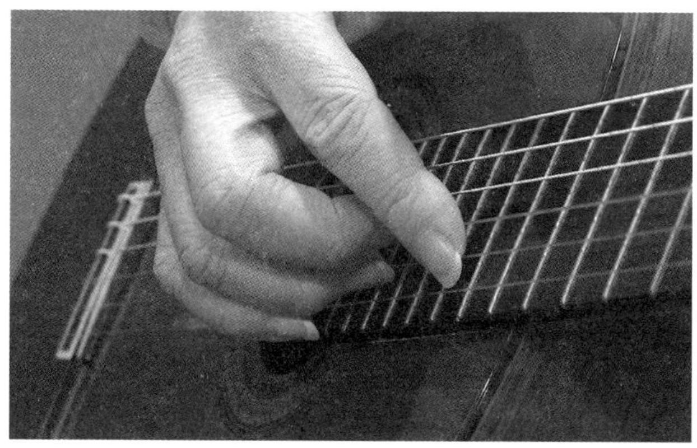

To master the technique, practice this extended one-octave E major scale while watching your right hand and using conscious GDM. Memorize and practice it by itself first so that you can rely on the *feel* of the fingering while concentrating on accurate right-hand movements.

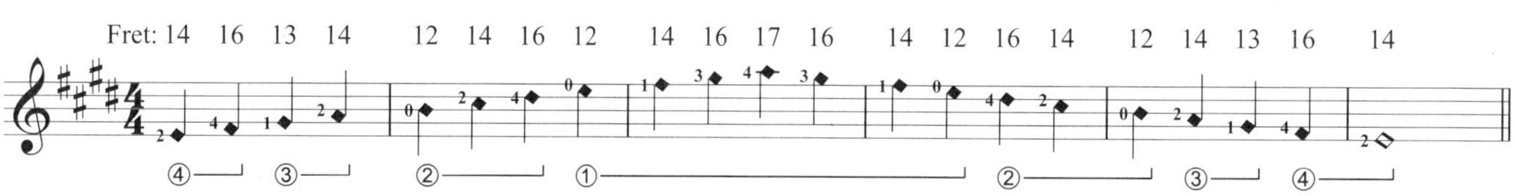

TIP: The secret of goal-directed point-and-pluck movements is to *lead* the pointing index finger with your eyes, as if they were *pulling* the fingertip to its destination over the right fret.

Treble-string harmonics can be combined with regular bass-string notes to create a charming music box sound. To support the melody without competing with it, play the bass notes very softly, using the fleshy left underside of your thumb-tip instead of the nail. This most famous of Christmas carols is ideally suited to the technique and will provide a good introduction to it.

TIP: Practice the piece without harmonics until it's well memorized, so that you can count on accurate left-hand movements while focusing your attention on the right hand's complex activity.

Silent Night

Franz Gruber
(1787–1863)

TREMOLO PLAYING

The last piece in this book, an original arrangement of "Greensleeves," will introduce you to the **tremolo** technique—the magical illusion of a duet between the guitar and an instrument like the mandolin which can sustain a continuous melody with fast up-and-down picking. However, like most magic tricks, there's a simple secret—basically, it's a *p-a-m-i* arpeggio in which *a, m,* and *i* play the *same* string. Therefore, your practice will need to focus squarely on the rotary cycle of consecutive right-hand preparations needed to create the illusion. Practice it thoroughly with deliberate sequential planting and staccato articulations as explained on pages 9, 32, 56, and 64. Look for those sensations of your fingers feeling chained together and sticking to the strings as evidence that you're practicing effectively.

Practicing Tremolo for Control Without Aggressive Planting

When the piece is memorized and you can play it at 108 BPM or faster, practice it also with two *reflex-based* modes of dynamic preparation:

[1] With the dotted rhythm shown:

[2] As written, but by accenting *m* with a more forceful stroke than the *a* stroke.

These two practice techniques will check the universal tendency of tremolos to "gallop" as they approach the entirely reflex-based performance speed, by closing the neuromuscular gap between well-controlled playing and accurate reflex playing.

Greensleeves

Traditional English
Arr. Charles Duncan

Andante Grazioso M.M. ♪ = 126–138

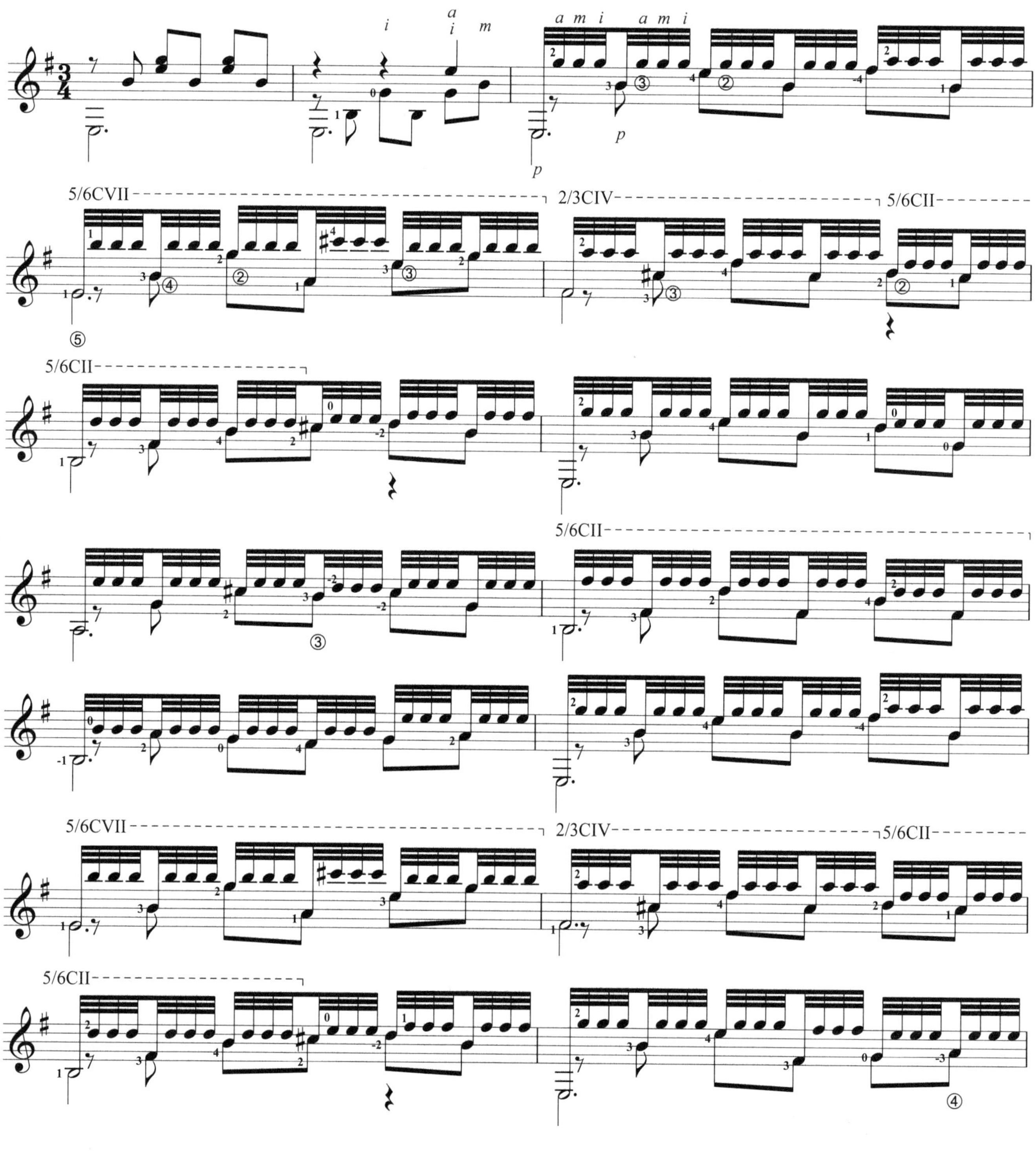

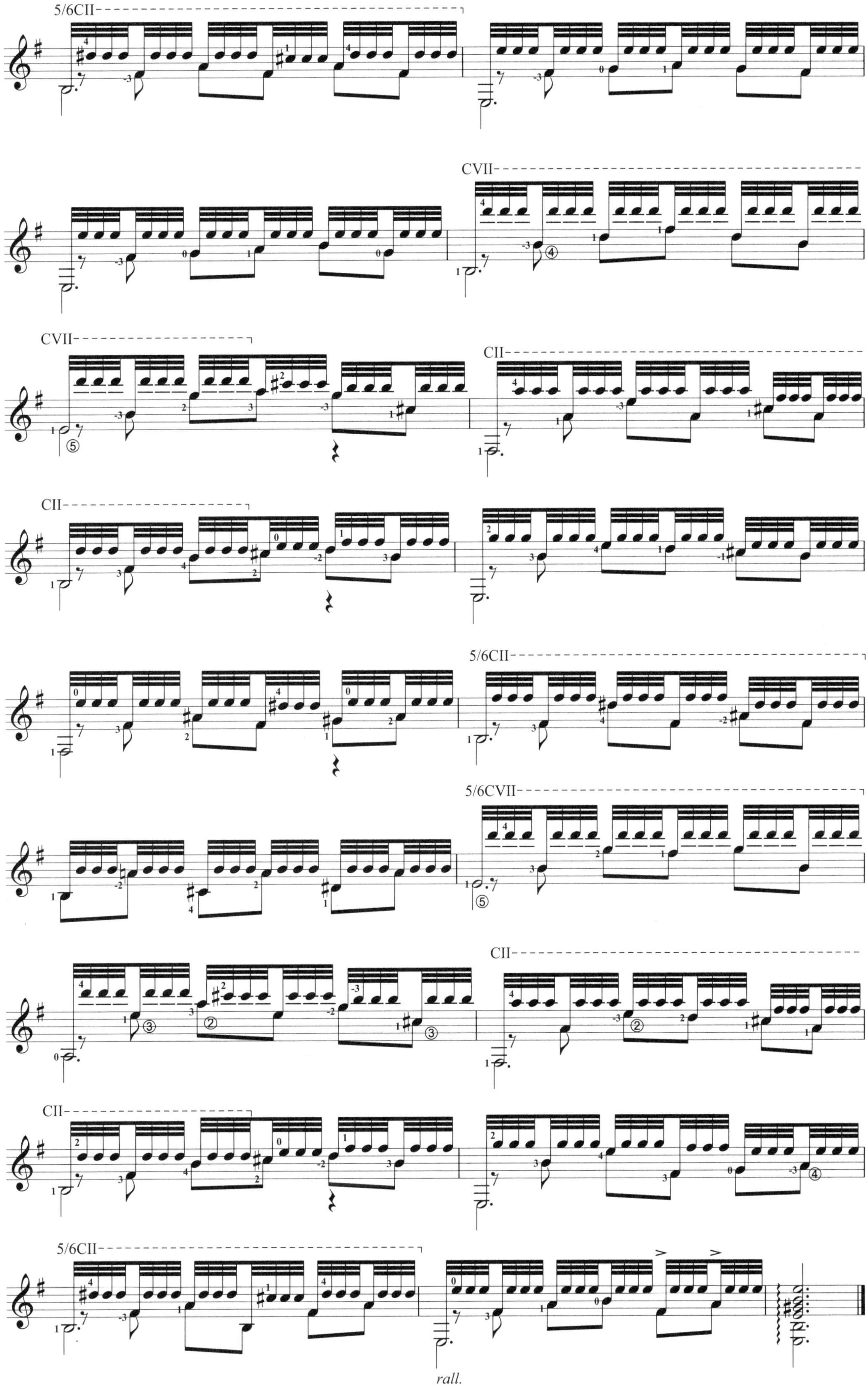
5/6CII
CVII
CVII
CII
CII
5/6CII
5/6CVII
CII
CII
5/6CII
rall.

Continuing Your Study

Students who have completed this book should be ready to start exploring the advanced guitar repertoire. Of the various ways to do this, the best would be to use some standard anthologies of etudes as a bridge to the highest levels. The following widely used classics are recommended:

(1) **Required Studies for Classical Guitar**, ed. Jerry Willard (Hal Leonard, 2008). This comprehensive collection contains Mauro Giuliani's *120 Studies for Right-Hand Development*, as well as many other etudes and recital pieces by Carcassi, Sor, Carulli, and more. The Giuliani studies used on pp. 9–10 cover the essential styles of arpeggiation, but the sheer number and variety of Giuliani's arpeggio patterns is an asset. Working on just 10–15 a week on a rotating basis will keep your practice of arpeggios constantly refreshed.

(2) **Matteo Carcassi: 25 Melodious and Progressive Studies, op. 60**, ed. Paul Henry (Hal Leonard, 1993). Even after 175 years, this book retains its unique value as an instructional work. The etudes are enjoyable, the variety of techniques they cultivate is comprehensive, and their increasing levels of difficulty are well-designed to incentivize a student's progress.

(3) **Twenty Studies for the Guitar by Fernando Sor**, ed. Andrés Segovia (1947; Hal Leonard, 1995). This too is a classic which has withstood the test of time because of its editor's prestige and the musical excellence of the pieces selected. Since its overall level of difficulty is greater, this book provides a fine complement to Carcassi's. Both editions include high-quality recordings of the pieces.

(4) **Etudes Simples (Estudios Sencillos) for Guitar**, by Leo Brouwer (Editions Durand, 2016). For an introduction to modern and contemporary guitar music, this book is unbeatable. The 20 short compositions by one of the finest guitar composers of the late 20th century cover a range of styles (impressionistic, atonal, Afro-Cuban, etc.), and are both instructive and fun to play.

(5) **Villa-Lobos: Collected Works for Guitar**, by Heitor Villa-Lobos (Editions Durand, 2001). The guitar music of this great Brazilian composer is such an important part of the modern repertoire that you should begin learning some of it. Besides their intrinsic value, his pieces serve as a gateway to a vast amount of more recent guitar music. Since most of his *12 Etudes* are quite difficult, a better place to begin would be with the "Choro No. 1," "Etude No. 1," and "Prelude No. 1."

To these valuable works may be added the author's *A Modern Approach to Classical Guitar Repertoire, Part 2* (Hal Leonard, 1985) for a choice selection of intermediate-to-advanced pieces from the traditional repertoire. To learn more about flamenco, the *Hal Leonard Flamenco Guitar Method* by Hugh Burns is the first book to get. And to broaden your understanding of modern music and explore the techniques of jazz playing, the *Hal Leonard Jazz Guitar Method* by Jeff Schroedl is unsurpassed.

Finally, to pursue your technique development to the max, the author's *Classical Guitar 2000: Technique for the Contemporary Serious Player* (Summy Birchard Music, 1993) is highly recommended (see, for example, the Amazon reviews). With a complete, practical scale system, comprehensive slur and arpeggio studies, and exercises for interpretive control—all supported by a thorough explanatory text—it combines the best features of many other technique books into a convenient 91-page package. Also, like its companion volume *The Art of Classical Guitar Playing*, it contains various unique features which even after three decades are not found elsewhere.